MW00777239

Eloped the Mental Hospital with

The Whisper of God's Voice

Who Said Bipolar Disorder is Incurable?

Denise Torres

Masterpiece Press

New York, U.S.A

Edits by Meghana Wunnava

Manufactured in the United States of America

ISBN: 979-8-9861846-0-9
LCCN: 2022908782

ACKNOWLEDGEMENTS

I want to share my sincere gratitude to everyone who has crossed my path and helped me recover from my traumatic Divorce.

Thank you, God, for my parents who were handpicked just for me. I adore them for all the values, morals and life lessons they have instilled in me, which I hope to pass onto my children. I'm grateful I finally live closer to my two sisters in Florida.

I want to thank JoAnn who noticed I was out by myself one day at Insignia. She gestured to me from across the room to join her for a drink with her lovely spouse, brother, and girlfriend. These small acts of kindness make a difference in people's lives. I have been blessed because no matter where life took me, people noticed me and new friendships were fostered. Even today, I feel pleasantly surprised each time I'm noticed. When you see someone who looks like they're by themselves, try to include them in your circle. You never know how you will impact their life with a simple gesture of kindness.

I want to thank Allen who played a pivotal role in my recovery from my trauma. He helped me restore my relationship with my two boys when I thought I was too broken to enjoy a healthy rapport with them.

I want to thank Ryan who constantly made me laugh and bridged the other gaps of my life to help me push through. You were my best companion during COVID, respecting my boundaries of no sex until marriage. My whole family thanks you for all your support.

Lastly, I want to thank my bestie, Virginia, for directing me towards a more promising future outside of New York that I couldn't envision for myself. You helped me see past my own shortcomings.

For everyone else I didn't mention, just being able to display the fun memories on my Facebook pages says it all. I call it, "Fake Book." I'm as transparent as they come with a delightful smile. Fake it till you make it with promising faith. Behind every smile, each of us carries significant burdens. It still pains me to leave all the people who have touched my heart. I can't wait for the next chapter of my life. My story is for God's Glory. Please continue to keep me in your prayers.

Thank you, Lord, for your whisper directed at my heart, "I have something far greater than all three of those relationships." I thought to myself, *who's the third person?* I was only thinking about Ryan and Anthony. So, I know it was God's small whisper. Perhaps it could have been Allen who came to my rescue when I was paralyzed and didn't even want to get out from underneath the sheets. Or it could have been Aziz, whose phone number I still had memorized and who helped me immensely after I was discharged from the hospital. The third person isn't important, I thought to myself. I had a great chuckle just knowing God is telling me, why settle for less when I know your value better than you know yourself. I'm patiently waiting for the Lord to finish writing my story.

This book is dedicated to
my two sons Luke and Jake.
I want you to know I gave it my all
to have custody over you munchkins.
I trust God can still restore what I lost one day.

Table of contents

MEMOIR

For those of you who don't know me, I'm a social introvert with many acquaintances because I like to avoid drama. I love being surrounded by people, but I also need my alone time to recharge. There is nothing I enjoy more than my own company as my solitary moments allow me to persevere in my faith. While I graciously danced through the pain, the people who have crossed my path have gradually helped me heal.

I was born and raised a Catholic on November 28, 1975. I graduated from Hofstra University with a BA in Business Computer Information Systems. I took an elective class in Jewish studies and my faith evolved when I began reading the Torah. When I initiated my relationship with Christ, I got baptized at the Centerpoint Church at the age of 26. Being baptized was my way of telling God I want to leave my old ways behind and follow the Lord to the best of my ability being perfectly imperfect.

When I was just 25 years old, I started my own business venture incorporating Wig Boutique. I purchased my first home four years later as a single women. I was well accomplished. Paid cash for a Volvo Convertible and travelled around to witness the beauty that the world has to offer. I didn't feel the need to get married as I was very independent and living my best life. But then I met Robert, who charmed me over with chivalry and his knowledge of scripture. I ignored the various red flags that kept propping up and got married at 29. Two years later I had my first son, Louis. Even though I was well accomplished, I still didn't feel successful. While pregnant I joined MLS Libor as a realtor to supplement my income. I passed my exam and sold a few houses. Two years after Louis, God surprised me with Jonathan. After ten years of marriage, everything fell apart despite countless attempts to restore it through counseling sessions, Christian marriage retreats, and Bible-based prayer groups. I must have read every self-help book I could find in Barnes and Noble and Amazon. On Halloween, I closed my business as sales began to plummet. Three days later, I was admitted involuntarily into a psychiatric ward based on false allegations. I refused experimental research and eloped from the psychiatric facility. I found the strength to escape from my marriage as well. I had $10k in my business bank account which helped me afford a retainer of $7,500 for my divorce attorney. I stayed in five-star hotels to pretend as though I was on a vacation. Eventually my funds began to deplete and I had to stay in motels as I remained waitlisted for housing in a shelter. Since I fled from the psychiatric ward, I lost my house and my children. In this short period of time, I reopened my business and honed my social media marketing skills; updated my website with the computer skills learned from Hofstra University which never left me.

My divorce was finalized after two years. What started in the Supreme Court, moved to a grueling Trial. Just when I thought it was over, my ex-husband thought he was still in the ring with me. I was notified to meet Robert at the Appellate Court. How could he afford this long-drawn battle, I wondered. Robert had a family friend attorney on his side. How did I afford this? In hindsight, I don't even know. I just told the Lord to fill my jars with oil to pay my debts and I can live on what is left over like he did for the widow women in 2 Kings 4:1-7. The Appellate Court directed us to go back to the Supreme Court. Family Court did not expedite the process either. What a dance. But thankfully, there was one silver lining- the divorce settlement helped me win my house back. The house I purchased before marriage, thankful his name was not on the deed.

I came dangerously close to losing the house I purchased before marriage. But life took a harsh turn nonetheless, as I lost custody of my children. I wasn't going to give up my children that easily. I was allowed restricted supervised visits of only three hours a day per week. I remained relentless and finally got two days a week after five years of my pursuit for justice at the Family Court, Supreme Court, and Appellate Court. I hired the best lawyers and spent every dime I had to win and even accumulated substantial debt. So, I lift my head high to the sky and give thanks because my God did not fail me. His grace is sufficient for me, 2 Corinthians 12:9. After five exasperating years my credit cards were finally paid off.

When the devil tries to make me lose my faith in God, it only draws me closer to my father Jesus Christ. 2 Corinthians 12 says, "My grace is sufficient for you, for my power is made perfect in weakness." I thank the Lord every day for helping me weather the storms that always draw me closer to him. Job 40:6, "the Lord spoke to Job out of the storm." I never want to miss the whisper of God's voice. I can only persevere knowing Jesus comforts me. Never stop praying, however long it takes. Stay strong and never lose faith!

"Remember when the furious storm comes, even the winds and the waves obey him!"

—   Matthew 8:24-27

INTRODUCTION

To all the married and single women out there, remember this: Happiness is a choice. I remember being married and still feeling lonely. Even after I had children, I still grappled with loneliness, since my two sisters lived in Florida and we lived in New York. My kids wouldn't grow up with their cousins. My oldest sister lived locally, but was estranged from all of us. She lived a busy elaborate lifestyle that was only conducive for herself. My husband worked seven days a week and I felt like a single parent. He refused to take off for Easter to spend time with us. On holidays, it felt lonely not having a large family to feast with. Eventually, I silenced the voices that screamed of my loneliness and sought contentment with my small family of two boys and my husband. Shortly after my marriage began to fall apart because of my meddling in-laws, blocked phone access raising suspicions of Robert's infidelity, and his lack of any desire for intimacy. Being single can also feel like a lonely place at times, but I have learned to love my solitude with my sweet Jesus.

I've recently had people tell me I'm always happy and they love my energy (I call it the Holy Spirit). However, they have no knowledge of my internal struggles. I remind myself that *emotions are not facts.* The Holy Spirit within me is what keeps my emotions in check. I memorized Jeremiah 17:7 8. "But blessed is the one who trusts in the Lord, whose confidence is in him." Make no mistake; I wrestle with God just like Jacob did in Genesis 32:24-28 until he received his blessing. We too are called to be overcomers of our circumstances.

Every morning, I choose to be happy. Not always easy to fake the funk but I always believed in *"fake it till you make it."* The same way I fake my confidence by wearing wigs. You're allowed to be happy even in your pain. It takes far more energy to stay angry than to be cheerful. Proverbs 17:22 says, "A cheerful heart is good medicine, but a crushed spirit dries up the bones."

I found healthy ways to heal my broken heart. I find joy in jogging the preserves, participating in 5K runs, bike riding, hiking, kayaking, and attending bible study groups to grow my faith. Therapy is helpful to understand my emotions that sometimes gets the best of me. John 10:10 says, "the thief comes to steal and kill and destroy; I have come so they may have life and have it to the full," I will enjoy my life under all circumstances.

I may have a thorn in my side like Paul in the Bible did, but I thank God, as it keeps me reliant upon the Lord; otherwise I would be lost. Remember to choose happiness. Happiness is a mindset. Happiness begins with self-love and valuing only your acceptance of yourself and that of God's. Remember, God is love and no one will love you more than him. Stop seeking love in all the wrong places; seek God himself. Otherwise, you will find yourself even emptier than a shell. Wrestle with your emotions with Jesus by your side and watch the blessings that will be bestowed upon you.

CHAPTER ONE

HOW I FELL IN LOVE WITH JESUS AND THEN SHORTLY AFTER MET MY FIANCÉ.

When you are single, you want to be married. When you are married, you want to be single. Relationships have their peaks and valleys. Finding the person who will weather the storm with you when you're in the valley should be the end goal. Who wants to date the nice guy you're not attracted to? I sure don't. I dated an unattractive guy, with a big heart, to discover even they are capable of cheating on you.

I was dating a guy, Stephan, who was healthy, never smoked, was tall and built like an ox. But as we all know, life often throws unpleasant surprises - he got diagnosed with lung cancer. While I always considered him a good friend, he relentlessly pursued me for a serious relationship before his diagnosis. My disinterest in Stephan stems from his occasional mentions of an ex-girlfriend who broke his heart. I'm not particularly fond of rebounder guys. We started out as friends first, but I was compelled to be his girlfriend in light of the bad news to reassure him I wasn't leaving his side.

My visits at Stephan's would typically involve playing board games and watching movies together. However, during each of these visits, his mother would begin acting territorial as though I was invading her personal space. During one such instance, she entered the room and began massaging Stephan's shoulders, which seemed particularly strange to me. *Couldn't she do this when I leave?* I ignored her actions, understanding her son was sick.

I hoped that our relationship would function as a healthy distraction, he was understandably mentally consumed by the illness. The disappointment of not being given enough time to live must have caught him off guard and made him feel like he was already dead and defeated. I, for one, refused to believe the doctors' prognosis. They are not God; he could outlive the one year of expectancy they had so statistically proclaimed. The fact is that, with or without cancer, we cannot take tomorrow for granted. I'm grateful to just wake up each morning. I don't allow circumstances to engulf me or drive me into misery. Empathy is not my strongest trait, as even in the worst moments of my life, I'm still optimistic. I'm more sympathetic because I don't want to swim in the other person's emotions. While I was truly sorry about his illness, I couldn't relate to his circumstances. Cancer to me doesn't mean death. To me cancer means survivor. I embrace life's challenges as an overcomer to be a supportive example to others. I dealt with my own life with healthy distractions, jogging, reading, journaling, and praying. I suppose I masked most of my grief and focused on ensuring that others were okay. I remember when I underwent a c-section, I was instructed to stay in bed. Yet, I tried to serve my visitors a three-course meal after a major surgery. I put others' concerns over my own comfort.

I wanted Stephan to look beyond the cancer so I encouraged him to call me more frequently. It seemed as though if I didn't call, he would not have initiated it. At this point, I contemplated if I was better off devoting my energy somewhere other than this relationship. I then registered at Hofstra University for a computer graphics class in Adobe Photoshop to distract myself from my own discomfort. Depression clouded Stephan's comprehension of what I was communicating. In my opinion, I was asking for the bare minimum but gradually, my motivation to visit someone who just wanted to feel defeated was fading. I felt helpless because I couldn't help him snap out of his negative thoughts to stay in the present. Worry has never been a part of my DNA. From childhood, whenever I would sustain any injuries and cry, my mother would tell me, "Don't worry, you're fine." My mother never worried much, and I essentially inherited that trait. If worry does creep into my mind, I remind myself Matthew 6:25-27 which says, "Therefore, I tell you, do not worry about your life, what you will eat or drink; or about your body, what you will wear. Is not life more important than food, and the body more important than clothes? Look at the birds of the air; they do not sow or reap or store away in barns, and yet your Heavenly Father feeds them. Are you not much more valuable than they? Who of you by worrying can add a single hour to his life?" Usually what we fear doesn't even transpire. I desperately wanted my old friend Stephan back.

As I discussed this situation with my work friend Angela, she stated that men aren't too bright so an analogy might help. She said, "Tell him you're like a plant and he needs to water you so you can grow." I immediately called Stephan and shared the analogy so our relationship can flourish. When I went home and opened up my Bible, I automatically turned to page 1 Corinthians 3:6, "I planted the seed, Apollos watered it, but God made it grow. So, neither he who plants nor he who waters is anything, but only God who makes things grow." I was flabbergasted. Who knew the Bible had verses concerning plant-watering. I told Angela about the Bible verse I discovered and asked, "Are you familiar with this verse, because your analogy is similar?" She said, "No, I don't know scripture. It was an advice that came from my heart." This must have been the Holy Spirit within her talking without her realizing it. I was dumbfounded. I was not acquainted with the Bible myself except for what I learned through Jewish studies at Hofstra University as an elective class. I was always fascinated with religion. I also took Greek mythology in my college years and wrote a thesis comparing Pandora's Box to Adam and Eve. Pandora's curiosity led her to open a box that was forbidden, thus releasing physical and emotional curses upon mankind. And Adam and Eve both ate the apple out of curiosity because it was forbidden in Genesis 3:1-17. Both stories allowed temptation to get the best of them. I don't think the teacher liked my perspective because I received a C minus, even though I thought it was an extremely impressive comparative paper. Perhaps my grades reflected how I felt about myself- not smart. I absorbed so much knowledge in my college years despite mediocre grades. However, I will never regret attending. I needed the degree because my parents stressed on its importance. I was more concerned with making money. However, I am so glad my parents encouraged me to attend college and become a well-rounded person.

After the conversation with Angela, I realized that I just needed to plant the seed and God was going to take care of the growth. I knew Jesus was a carpenter and a fisherman, but I didn't know he was an amazing gardener as well. No matter how purposefully I tried, my plants never survived. Maybe I didn't talk to them enough. I became so consumed, spending every minute I could with Stephan, that it was time for me to replenish my needs before I wilt. I had attended a craft event with my sister Janice and met this lady selling handmade jewelry with earth stones. I was fascinated by her creative skills and products, so I splurged $75 on a custom piece of jewelry for myself. I knew it was overpriced, but I appreciated the handmade talent. The jewelry maker guided me towards a rock and she said, "This is a healing rock." My sister said, "Purchase it for Stephen. Maybe it could heal his lung cancer." I experienced uneasy negative emotions pertaining to the rock because only God holds the ability to heal. My sister insisted, so I purchased the rock. I told my mom about the jewelry maker who said, "It's a healing rock." But I knew it really wasn't. My mom told me, "Don't worry. God is in the rock, just give it to him." So that night when I went to visit him, I told him, "I bought this rock for you because the lady said it has healing powers; but I would prefer if you believed more in what you couldn't see. A miraculous healing is possible without a rock." Stephan, of course, accepted the rock.

When I went home to open my Bible, I randomly flipped to Hebrews 11, "Now faith is being sure of what we hope for and certain of what we do not see." Again, I couldn't believe this. These words emerged from my heart though I was unaware that my Holy Spirit spoke these very words that are written in the Bible. I was amazed but also skeptical if God was really communicating with me in this manner. Or was it just a coincidence? Was this the voice of God? John 10:27 says, "My sheep hear my voice, and I know them, and they follow me."

The next day, my dad told me that he was going to the St. Kilian Catholic Church because they are having a special service: washing of the feet. I thought to myself, *What is washing of the feet?* I randomly flipped to the page John 13:13–17, "Now that I, your Lord and teacher, have washed your feet, you also ought to wash one another's feet. For I have given you an example, that you should do as I have done to you." This passage is a good reminder to stay humble. We are never too important to serve others. I couldn't believe it. Once again, God answered my question. This happened too many times to dismiss it as a coincidence. God reciprocates communication when I silently speak to him. I immediately conveyed to God that I wanted him to speak to me every day and bless me with his presence. It took me a while to realize he wanted a very simple relationship with us. So many people focus on traditions, religious chants, and laws, while completely neglecting the friendship part of our relationship with God, who loves us.

A few days later, I communicated to God my interest in learning to read the Bible. The very next day Thomas, a vendor, approached me and asked, "Ava, would you want to check out Centerpoint Church in Massapequa? I think you would like it. It's a young congregation." I knew I had to attend a church other than that of Roman Catholic, because it did not invigorate my spirituality. Most of the church-goers at St. Kilian were elderly. The missile or service book fell short of explaining the true meaning of the Bible. Wow! Again, God was quick to resolve my predicament. I didn't know Thomas was a Christian and the invitation caught me by surprise. I only knew Thomas as the food vendor from my workplace. Thomas hardly ever spoke to me barring a polite "hello" and a "goodbye." I replied to his invitation expressing my search for a place where I could enjoy understanding the Bible.

When I attended the Centerpoint Church for the first time, I felt the messages being directed right at me. The sermon was clear clarification of questions I had been inquisitively wondering about. This birthed my love for Jesus. God's words inadvertently touched my heart. Since this recurred frequently, I knew not to dismiss my newfound relationship with my heavenly Father.

Stephan wasn't too thrilled about my newfound love for Jesus. I, on the other hand, was excited to introduce him to the verses that jumped from the pages of God's biblical truths. I so desperately wanted Stephan to understand me. Instead, he probably thought I was a fanatical weirdo. I continued to go to every Slomin's Kettering Hospital visit in NYC and my non-denominational Christian faith church. I realized I wasn't following a religion; I'm focusing on my relationship with Christ. Soon, I was baptized.

My parents didn't want to attend my baptism and asserted that they had already baptized me in the Catholic faith. They were unsupportive of my decision. My dad approached me and sarcastically said, "I suppose you found yourself another father." I just laughed and replied, "How did you know?" My younger sister, Raquel, disagreed with my new lifestyle but still stood in support to attend my baptism.

I wept like a baby when I shared my testimony and then the pastor immersed me into the pool of water. I felt cleansed of my sins and I received the gift of the Holy Spirit within me, as referenced in Acts 2:38. Did you know Jesus was baptized by John at the Jordan River (Luke 3:21-23) at the age of 30 and the Holy Spirit descended on him? Luke 3:22 says, "And a voice came from heaven; "You are my Son, whom I love; with you I am well pleased." Today, I call on the Holy Spirit within me for guidance on a regular basis. Without its directions, I would feel utterly lost in this world. I need to hear the whispers of God's gentle voice.

The next day I told Stephan that I wanted to just be friends with him because I didn't feel the love in the relationship anymore. I did, however, promise to continue going to all his hospital visits. He was very understanding. I'm sure he didn't want to date a fanatical girl with a newfound faith anyway. I had prayed to God that I'm satisfied being single with my newfound love for Jesus. But if God wanted to send me a good partner as a bonus, I would be celibate until marriage. Not that I was a virgin, but I desired to be obedient to what was required of me by my Father in Heaven- to avoid sexual immorality outside of marriage, as stated in 1 Corinthians 7:12. My only request to God was to send me someone who is God-fearing, has green eyes, is Spanish, and looks European. My list was pretty short. But little did I know that when you pray to God for a little, you will be gifted with just that- a little. Don't make my mistake. Perhaps I felt undeserving and didn't want to seem selfish by requesting too much. Now I ask for the unimaginable because Luke 1:37 says, "nothing is impossible with God."

My childhood friend, Virginia, invited me to attend her Christian church. At first, I was uncomfortable because of the unfamiliar charismatic nature of the church. I had never experienced anything like that before, which can be attributed to my Catholic background. I heard someone speaking in an unknown language during worship, which was called "speaking in tongues." I had never witnessed anything like that. I didn't you can just blurt out in the middle of a sermon. I wasn't sure what was the right moment to consume the wine and the bread that was handed to me. I was accustomed to forming a queue and taking bread directly from the pastor. At the end of the service, a guy named Robert approached us because he thought he knew Virginia. He introduced himself with his Spanish nickname Gringo which translates to white boy. He happens to be Columbian. He had green eyes. He perfectly fit my criteria. Virginia invited him to the diner we were headed towards. Robert joined us and enquired about my line of work. A week later he visited my store at Wig Boutique and invited me to a Christian banquet dinner fundraiser for Teen Challenge. Robert impressed me by generously tipping the guy who seated us at the coliseum. He would always open the car door for me. Sometimes, I rushed out of the vehicle, unaccustomed to such chivalry. He was a romantic, whereas I was more pragmatic. He would find the perfect hallmark cards and surprise me with the most thoughtful gifts. Robert would randomly leave me money in the glove box of my car in case of emergencies. He was well-versed with the etiquettes of chivalry and respected my religious boundaries of celibacy until marriage.

Robert didn't own a car at the time because he was the supervisor of the men's home at the Teen Challenge rehabilitation center. I didn't know much about the program except that Robert was residing at the Christian residential care center for young people and adults battling addiction. He was the supervisor of the men's home that was a center for individual and group biblical studies, work projects, and recreation. His tendency to help others was particularly attractive and I noticed that even the children took a liking to him. When we first met, Robert was clean three years after overcoming his addictions. Since Robert didn't have a car, I would pick him up and drop him off. His curfew was in no way a hurdle, since I grew up with a similar home structure and rules. I never imagined I would be escorting him and seeking permission to date him through the program he was involved in. When I sat down with one of the program coordinators, I jokingly asked if they needed my resume. Apparently, they didn't think it was funny. In return, I got grilled with a few personal questions about my background. How we met, if I attended church, what denomination I practiced, and so forth. How did this script get twisted? I thought the ritual was for the man to get the blessings from the parents to date. I was lucky enough to have parents that allowed me to choose my boyfriends and learn from my own mistakes. My parents raised me and my three sisters with strict discipline and work ethic. It was easy for me to understand when you're under someone else's roof there are rules to be followed until you can stand on your own two feet. Since Robert was supervising the program and was provided with accommodation, there were rules he had to follow. I respected that.

My sister's boyfriend Stuart looked up Robert's criminal record and shared it with my parents. They had no clue Robert had felonies and freaked out. Till date, I'm unsure about why Stuart thought it was necessary to get involved in my personal life. Robert had multiple charges of assault, drug possession and theft. My family was not thrilled about me marrying an ex-convict with no college degree, who was also a recovered addict. I disregarded his previous background because I believe people can change. I, perhaps, was looking for a converted bad boy who already got everything out of his system and has finally found Christ. But little did I know what I was getting into! Later, towards the end of our marriage, he shared I was more of a fanatic and he confessed that we were not on the same page as I had thought.

Robert's family didn't want to welcome anyone into their small family circle. When Robert and I started dating more frequently, he couldn't wait to introduce me to his family. Robert spoke highly of me to them. Every time we were scheduled to visit his younger sister Julie, she would find an excuse. Once, she cancelled the plan claiming she wasn't feeling well. Another time, she stated that we couldn't just drop by her house unannounced in case she wasn't dressed. Who walks around naked in their home in the afternoon or evening? Unless she wanted to make sure she had her runway gown on for me.

Another time, she said we couldn't stop by because she was expecting company. They didn't seem like excuses initially. However, when it happened repeatedly, I realized her actions were intentionally avoidant of my acquaintance. Through Robert, she invited me to her daughter's birthday party, where we would finally meet. I was working that day, but I knew it was important to Robert, so I took the day off. She didn't inform Robert of the party venue.

On the day of the party, he called her several times but she didn't pick up. After the party ended, she said, "Michael, why didn't you come to the party?" I shared my assumption with Robert, "Perhaps she doesn't want to meet me." I don't think he wanted to believe that. She was very calculated in her manipulation. She was an amazing actress. I'd give her an Oscar. I had an intuition that I was being snubbed.

One afternoon Julie told Robert, "Why don't you and Ava come over and babysit my two boys and daughter." I was happy to oblige. This would be my first acquaintance with her. When we arrived at her house, Julie had a surprise birthday cake waiting for me. She filmed me blowing out the candles on her camcorder while they sang 'Happy Birthday.' It seemed like a very thoughtful gesture, which I expressed to Robert. I never had anyone throw me a surprise party. She ordered pizza and then went on her date with her husband. *Okay, so perhaps she does like me,* I thought.

The next day, Robert conveyed to me that Julie didn't think I looked happy, and stated that the video was proof of that. She even offered to play it back for him. She was definitely imaginative. Never in my wildest dreams could I invent such a story. I told Robert, "How could I have looked unhappy when I reiterated how much I enjoyed the party?" I think it was easier for Robert to just be in denial to avoid conflict. I didn't want to be involved in any type of drama myself. I had to let this go.

Since Robert and I were considering marriage he was going to look for a job outside of Teen Challenge while still volunteering to help others as a mentor. I found it interesting that his mother and sister wanted Robert to be codependent on them, but didn't want Robert to leave Teen Challenge nor live with them. My Aunt allowed Robert to rent a room at my cousin Isabelle's house instead. It seemed as though his sister and mother were not fond of the idea of Robert furthering his career. His sister and mother preferred Robert living and working for the teen challenge program because they didn't want to relinquish their control over his life and his whereabouts. Or maybe, they were doubtful of his ability to make it on his own. Robert found a job delivering used auto parts.

As an entrepreneur, I later encouraged him to start his own business in the auto parts industry. But I soon discovered that, in life, not everyone is equipped with the skills to be an entrepreneur. It requires a whole different mindset. You must be willing to take on high risks to get high rewards and be prepared for failure to help you succeed higher. Anything I suggested, he opposed. He probably thought I was trying to control him. He didn't want to hire employees. He didn't want a website. He didn't want to get an Astro van to advertise his business. Robert just enjoyed freelancing on his own schedule, while I was burdened with the responsibility of sustaining our family comfortably.

I had given Robert my Nissan Maxima. I went and purchased a Volvo C70 convertible in cash. Robert disclosed to me that his mother had money she was saving for him, so he wouldn't spend it for any kind of debauchery. But now, his mother was holding a tight fist and didn't want to relinquish his money. I told Robert that he could purchase my Nissan Maxima instead of borrowing my car. His mother didn't like the idea of Robert purchasing my car and made sure Robert's brother-in-law found him a used vehicle that was valued cheaper than the funds she was holding onto. I was not bothered by that. She was rude enough to tell Robert that I wouldn't get book value for my car, which was my offer for Robert to purchase the vehicle. In retrospect, I'm thankful for her meddling because I got more money for my car. What I want you readers to understand is that when people try to hurt you, they're actually blessing you. So, I wasn't upset. At the moment it may not look like a blessing because you're only noticing the devious behavior and intentions behind their actions. I'm a businesswoman, so the outcome was in my favor. That doesn't excuse her animosity toward me for trying to help her son.

Shortly after, I started looking for a house. I wanted the life my parents had. I knew investing in real estate was the only way to accomplish that. I walked into a real estate office in my local village and the realtor recommended this house in Bethpage. When I went to see it, I immediately fell in love with the house because it was a corner property. The house needed major Tender

Loving Care (TLC). The backyard resembled a forest. The house had asbestos shingles. Paneling in the living room. Carpeting in the kitchen. Yes, carpeting. The bathtub and toilet were pink, a specific shade that was probably used in the 50s. The wood flooring throughout the house was probably the only thing that I left unchanged. The vision I had for this house was something no one else could envision.

At the time, it was a seller's market. I just loved the neighborhood and knew from the minute I landed my eyes on the house that I wanted to live there. My dad told me to make a lowball offer on the property. I said, "No way. I want this house. I don't want someone else to outbid me." I offered $15k less than the asking price, although I was scared of jeopardizing my opportunity to get the house.

The next day I found out someone else outbid me. I cried, "Lord this was my house. I wanted it." I couldn't find any other house in that neighborhood going for that price. My father regretted giving me advice that went wrong. Everything else on the market was out of my price range.

Two days later, I picked up my head and said to myself, "Okay Lord, you must have something better for me." The agent took me to see two other houses and I didn't feel anything. Just more disappointment. Two weeks went by and she called me, "Ava, the investors who were going to buy the house you wanted just backed out of the deal." I cried again. I couldn't believe it. I didn't even have to increase my offer. Once again, my father in heaven came through for me. I was ecstatic.

My parents were concerned I was going to put my fiancé's name on the house. He was going to be my husband, so I didn't think twice before putting his name on the contract, despite my parents' disapproval. Robert recently received a settlement check from a personal injury accident as a passenger and collected $20k. Robert told me I can use it toward whatever I needed it. I put $40k down on the house and I deposited his $20k in the bank as an emergency fund. When we went for the closing of the house, Robert came with me and we both signed all the papers. My sister Raquel gave me a Tiffany pen as a house-warming gift, which I used to sign the deed. I treasured that pen.

Planning the wedding was a complete nightmare. My sister-in-law interfered at every step, telling me how to cross my T's and dot my i's literally. Julie didn't want her wedding invitation to read Mr. & Mrs. Perez. I was instructed, "The invitation should read Aunt Julie, Uncle Mark, Nephew Simon, Mark Jr. and Niece Alexa." I obliged. I made a quick Avery sticker label. I had to know when to pick and choose my battles. It was just easier to avoid confrontation. I really didn't know how to fight any battles. It was just simpler to keep the peace and stay quiet. But inside my head, I was agitated. *She is out of her mind. Whatever makes her happy just to keep the peace between us,* I thought. It wasn't much trouble anyhow. I didn't realize her demands would only get more ridiculous with time.

One day, Robert's mother Lola asked me, "Why did you send the Christmas card to Florida?" I was so confused, I thought to myself, *Did she move? Did she have a dual residence I didn't know about?* Robert himself was unsure if she was coming to

New York for the holidays. So, I had to be more strategic so Lola couldn't find any more flaws. The following year I sent a holiday card to her Florida residence and New York, where her daughter resides. I was soon catching onto her drama, constantly playing the victim card, as if I had a personal vendetta against her. I replied, "I didn't know you were going to be in New York for the holidays because of your health issues." Sometimes, Lola would claim she had ailments and everyday could be her last day. Robert told me that his grandmother was a hypochondriac, which led me to believe Lola was following the same pattern. All I know is that if you wish for anything in your life you may eventually manifest it. So, her lie can eventually be her truth.

My problems didn't end there. I was also blamed for sending an invitation to Lola and her husband, when they were no longer together. I was accused of deliberately putting both their names on the Surprise 40th Birthday invitation for Robert. I don't pry into people's relationships. This was Lola's second marriage. So I assumed if she came to New York alone, that perhaps her husband was spending time with his children from his first marriage. To be honest, I didn't ask questions because it doesn't concern me. I was confronted by Julie directly with "How dare you send an invitation to my mom and her husband, as if you didn't know they're not together any longer." She caught me off guard and I told her, "When people fight doesn't mean it's over. I'm sorry about the separation but I really had no clue." I asked Robert if he was aware they were separated. We were both clueless. Yet Robert stated that I should have known better as though I had a telepathic gift I didn't know about. He gave me too much credit to be so talented.

They wanted to see me in a downward dog position. I knew I would have to get in my warrior pose position instead, meditate on scriptures, and just breathe. At the same time, they were stretching my tolerance and stimulating my blood flow. I'm more intentional with my breathing when I'm in an uncomfortable position during hot yoga. Similarly, breathing needs to be more intentional in my life to regroup my thoughts. Actions undertaken out of anger often escalate the situation. It was easier to remain quiet. I'm not very aware of my breathing most of the time until I'm put in a stressful situation. Thank God for the autonomic nervous system which is responsible for sending signals to the circulatory system to ensure proper blood circulation and respiration. Once I can breathe, I can think logically. The jogs at night kept me sane and forced me to breathe. The bursts of anger gave me a rush of energy that I needed to release, recharge, and regroup.

My cousin Isabelle shared with me that she too would have been acting like Robert's sister, Julie because her perspective was basically, "What do you want with my brother?" What my cousin Isabelle and Julie had in common was that they wanted to be the ones responsible for helping their brothers and catering to their needs. They didn't want anyone else contributing to their success. They were codependent enablers not wanting to relinquish their control. These were undoubtedly selfish motives. Why wouldn't they appreciate someone else trying to alleviate some of the burden? Especially when that person can potentially be a positive influence in their lives. I can't decipher their thought process. All I know is Isabelle despised me from childhood, because I had a wealthier, more solid upbringing. I tried my best to treat her like my sister. I didn't judge her, so why did I have to be judged? I understand that when people are hurting, they want to hurt others. I couldn't imagine wanting to hurt my family members.

In high school, Isabelle's Puerto Rican best friend Gloria wanted to fight me without any valid reason. Girls in our school really didn't need a reason to put each other down. If you were pretty, they fought you. If you were quiet, they picked on you. If you were smarter, you were disliked or considered a nerd. The end denominator was if you had something they didn't have, you would have to defend yourself. A dog can sense emotions of fear and bullies were no different. I was told, "Gloria called you out." I could not comprehend what exactly that meant at the time. It meant a scheduled meeting after school to fight. Now if you don't show up, you look like a coward. Our so-called friends pushed us together and we fought. Gloria never bothered me again after that. Looking back, I wouldn't be surprised if Isabelle put her up to it. Especially since they were best friends.

I kept waiting for my husband to defend me to his mother and sister. I believed I needed him to intercede because it was his family. Robert would, after all, be better aware of how to handle them so they wouldn't dislike me. If my husband had an issue with my family, I would address the situation and actively work on a resolution, anticipating my family would listen to me. But apparently, Robert needed his mother and sister's approval just as much as I did. Therefore, neither of us would confront them.

If Robert did address them, he would tell them Ava said, "Bla bla bla" further fueling the   conflict. If only Robert was skilled at mediating a diplomatic outcome. 1 Timothy 2:5 says, *"For there is one God and one mediator between God and men, the man Christ Jesus, who gave himself as a ransom for all men."* This verse made me realize I don't need to go through anyone else to fight my battles, as Jesus is my direct connection to God. This is the reason I don't pray to Saints. The Lord didn't die on the cross on behalf of my sins so I can expect a miracle from someone else. I acknowledge and recognize all the Saints for the role they played in history, but I will never pray to them. I knew in my heart I could not use my husband as an intercessor either. Eventually I would have to find the courage to have a conversation and hope it doesn't turn into a confrontation. How could I expect my husband to confront my in-laws, when I didn't know how to do it myself?

The trigger of not being believed, protected, and noticed just kept haunting me. During confrontations, wrongdoers typically deflect the conversation, use reverse psychology, or even employ guilt-tripping tactics. I often walk away from them feeling unheard and unloved. If only Robert had simply validated my feelings by saying, "I know what they did was wrong, but please ignore them." I would have felt understood and protected. It was disgusting how my mother-in-law lived rent-free in my head. I would go to sleep and wake up angry because she would torment me in my nightmares. Until one day, someone told me I was idolizing my mother-in-law. I never realized I was mentally worshiping her. I have heard of worshiping money, fame, or a celebrity, but I didn't know that even negative attention toward a person can be an act of worship.

If I was not taking my hurt and pain and giving it to God, then I'm only hurting myself. I'm sure Lola slept like a log at night. Surely, I barely took up any space in Lola's head so why should I be bothered? Once I understood this, I started to pray for her. I began to tell Jesus, "Forgive me for worshiping anyone more than you. I bring my concerns to your feet and pray for my mother-in-law Lola. I don't understand why she wouldn't want to gain another daughter. I ask you, Lord, to heal her heart and pain with whatever is hindering our relationship. I can't get everyone to like me Lord, but I accept who I am in Christ." I will pray for my enemies as is required of us in Matthew 5:44; "But I tell you, love your enemies and pray for those who persecute you." I may not be a theologian, but I know enough scripture to help me power through the growing pains towards maturity. I could then, finally, comfortably rest my head at night.

CHAPTER TWO

RED FLAGS? SHOULD I CANCEL THIS WEDDING?

Just three months before the wedding, I began to have second thoughts. Our destination wedding was supposed to take place in the Dominican Republic, Punta Cana, Paradisus Palma Real Resort. I had consulted God on this matter. I implored him to conjure up a scenario where Robert would be required to defend me one more time against his mother and sister. If he did not stand up for me, I was ready to cancel this wedding. That very same day, Julie and her husband crashed Robert's surprise 40th birthday party although they initially denied my invitation, because Lola was in Florida and I planned it at the wrong time. I had given advanced notice to everyone. My immediate family didn't want to be there because Julie was very confrontational in the past. But, I reassured my parents relaying Julie's denial of the invitation. I even drove to Robert's local barber shop to invite several of the hair stylists to the surprise party. Robert knew them for a long time. I was certain he would be utterly surprised if they attend.he will be shocked when he sees them at his event. I was making certain that I met the minimum number of guests required, following Robert's sister and mother's refusal to come. I didn't want to cancel the brunch with the catering hall.

Yet, I was the one caught by surprise. Julie and her husband walked into the venue unexpectedly. I just remained calm and quiet. My family and I looked at each other, each visibly confused. My gut told me she came with an agenda because she arrived without her children. As long as she didn't ignite a flame, I knew it was best to let this slide. My parents were shocked and I explained to them that I was caught off-guard as well. I didn't want my family to be uncomfortable. But, the air was filled with undeniable tension.

Robert finally arrived at his surprise party, greeted everyone, and was immediately cornered by Julia who complained to him that I had excluded Julie's husband's family and Robert's friends who hadn't arrived yet. He believed his sister and not me. I immediately approached Julie and said calmly, "I thought you weren't coming?" She said, "I left you a message." I asked, "Oh really, how come I never received the message?" She immediately got out of her chair and stormed out with her husband. As she left, she said, "I don't need to be part of this faggot family." This was the green light to cancel the wedding right then and there. An event that was supposed to be celebratory, turned out to be a 4th of July explosion. I threw my phone at Robert and said, "If you don't believe me, check my phone. See if there is a message from her. She could have stayed and enjoyed the brunch. She came to do what she does best, stir drama." Robert believed she left me a voicemail and I may have deleted it. I canceled the wedding right then and there.

Shortly after, the guys from the barber shop arrived and Robert never got to blow out the candles. We didn't get past the cocktail hour. So, I thanked God for his signs and provision even during my storm. Later that night, Robert revealed that the cancellation of the wedding did not upset him. He was more upset he wasted his time dating me and we didn't even have sex. While

I was trying to be obedient to God, his intentions were obviously different, otherwise he wouldn't have been perturbed.

I had to take Robert's name off the purchase agreement of the house. Robert met me at my attorney's office and he signed his name off and I returned his $20k. The money wasn't tied to the investment of the home. Luckily, I had it readily available to return to Robert. At the signing, he bought me a beautiful clear glass plaque with a scripture verse engraved on it for me to have as a keepsake for my new home. He was always thoughtful like that. Too bad he just didn't know how to set boundaries with his sister and mother. They were free to keep him as they made my life miserable. I had lost the deposit on all the reserved hotel rooms for the accommodation of the guests at the Paradisus Palma resort. The personalized monogrammed robes for the guests were also non-refundable. I lost the money on the printed wedding invitations. I lost the deposit on my wedding gown. I was okay by all these losses, except for the tickets for Hawaii. I had the option of going alone because his ticket was non-transferable.

Now that I wasn't going to marry Robert, I sent his mother an email. I told her how I really felt because at this point it didn't matter if she liked me or not. I shared a dark secret Robert told me about her. *Hi Lola, I am no longer marrying your son. I just wanted to let you know I have returned the $20K back to Robert. You tried to talk poorly of Robert's dad when you got divorced. But that backfired because Robert resented you instead for sleeping with his dad's best friend while married. So apparently your daughter is following in your footsteps by trying to turn your* *son against me. Like mother, like daughter. The apple doesn't fall far from the tree. Just remember it always backfires.* She went ballistic after receiving this email. She told Robert she was going to call the cops on me. Not sure on what charges.

Ironically my pastor advised to take a break from each other for 30 days and his pastor's words were verbatim. I ended up traveling to India for exactly 30 days following the day I was supposed to get married. Yet again, God's guidance played an irrefutable role in all this. My mother met a gentleman from Bally's fitness who was looking for a business owner to engage in a cultural exchange program with the Rotary club. Rotary is a global network of 1.4 million neighbors, friends, leaders, and problem-solvers who see a world where people unite and take action to create lasting change – across the globe. The trip is completely paid for through the organization to discover another language, culture and truly become global citizens. I would be hosted in the homes of the Rotarians for exactly 30 days. I couldn't even make this up. God knows I love to travel and I needed to escape from Robert's incessant stalking. I frequently remind myself of God's goodness in my life even in the worst circumstances. These opportunities to travel are not what I actively sought; God just opened the doors knowing I love to explore.

When I returned from India, my ex-fiancé was still pursuing me. Robert promised to put an end to his family's meddling in our relationship. I didn't consult God to determine whether I should try to reconcile this relationship after all the red flags. I went out of God's will, and chose to believe Robert. Perhaps I thought I knew what I was doing. When I don't know what to do, I consult God. Meanwhile the lesson to learn is to consult God at every turn of your life. Robert and I publicly announced our decision to elope to Hawaii since his family disapproved this marriage. My parents were devastated. My family didn't do anything to be excluded from my matrimony. I just thought it was only fair to Robert to exclude my family also.

Robert's sister and mother decided to write Robert off for his continued desire to marry me. Julie viewed this occasion as a moment of losing her only brother, instead of perceiving it as gaining a sister-in-law. They didn't have any relatives in the United States and they were not ready to welcome anyone else in. It's unfortunate Julie didn't want an extended family, including her own spouse's family. Robert's dad Pablo told Robert, "If you love Ava, marry her because your sister Julie did the same to me. Julie tried to stop me from marrying my girlfriend."

My father-in-law dated this gorgeous, sophisticated Puerto Rican lady who was never married and never had children. She was an administrative assistant in New York City and dressed impeccably. Julie worked tirelessly to make sure her father would not marry or have children with any other women. Julie couldn't imagine her dad with children younger than her own. This didn't make sense to her. However, Julie made an allowance for her mother to remarry. My father-in-law couldn't risk not seeing his grandchildren, which was bound to happen if he went against Julie's wishes. This severed his relationship with his girlfriend. Julie's husband who is a devout Christian also told Robert, "If you love Ava, marry her because your sister has tried to alienate me too from my very own family."

During holidays, Julie would fly to Florida without her husband and spend Easter with her own mother and children to avoid spending time with her husband's side of the family. Finally, Robert admitted that Julies' actions were out of line and recited his father and brother-in-law's words. I trusted Robert enough to reconsider the engagement and just publicly elope to Hawaii since I still had the travel tickets. Robert then confessed that he had once married before, worried that his sister would disclose this to me one day. I was completely unaware.

Robert claimed that his sister sabotaged his previous marriage and all prior relationships he was in. He even presented to me all the documentation that confirmed his story. Just when you think you know someone! He also confessed that he was also married to another woman strictly for legal residency. He was paid $10k. Yet again, more red flags from his past were overlooked. This confirmed Robert was never oblivious of Julie's actions. He just didn't want me to be aware of her behavior, so he remained in denial.

Robert disclosed his guilt of substance abuse and how it affected his life. Robert was kicked out of private catholic school for misconduct. He came from a divorced home and this affected him. His mom tried to put Robert in Karate to help him with his anger issues but that didn't help. His mother would just drop him off and Robert would disappear from class. He truly believed that he would have enjoyed Karate if his mother took the time to watch him practice. I could understand that. She certainly was not a nurturing lady. She was too concerned about the vacuum marks on the floor and if they were all aligned in the same direction. Lola had a home similar to my mother's that didn't look lived in, almost like a showroom out of a magazine.

Julie had pleaded with Robert to stay out of trouble so he could attend her wedding. Unfortunately, he was unable to attend her wedding as he was imprisoned for selling stolen auto parts. When he was released, he still continued to hustle in the streets, drug dealing. Lola called the cops on her son because she felt he would be safer in prison than in the street. Robert was just following in his father's footsteps looking for acceptance. Pablo, at the time, had his own factory in NYC designing custom made suits and drug dealing on the side.

Robert's dad was constantly paying an exorbitant amount of money for various rehab facilities that were rendered ineffective. Julie asked Robert to be present at least for the birth of her first son. I suppose Robert didn't think he would get caught. Alas, he missed that special day of hers also. This pile-up of guilt was weaponized by his sister to control Robert. It's almost like he could never repay her for what he did in the past. So he would cover up her manipulative acts instead, almost like an accomplice. He probably blames himself for her actions. It was Julie's husband who visited Robert in prison and told him about the program Teen Challenge Christian based recovery program to help turn his life around.

I can't imagine how many people feel they could never be forgiven. Luckily, I understand when God forgives, he forgets.

Isaiah 43:25 says, "I, am he, who blots out your transgressions for my own sake, and I will not remember your sins."

Travel has always been my escape; my safe haven. I studied in Venice in my college years and visited Amsterdam where Anne Frank hid from the Nazis. She kept a diary, which is still remembered and widely read today. I love journaling as it helps me process my thoughts more clearly. I worked in London as an intern at Hamleys, which is the largest toy shop in the world. With seven floors full of toys, games, crafts and magic tricks. Many travelers around the globe came to visit this magical shop.

On my days off, I would take short trips to Paris, Ireland, and Italy. I continued traveling after college and had my younger sister Raquel join me. While I was dating Robert, I went to Spain with my sister Raquel which was a long-standing plan from before I met him. The fashionable elements of traveling fascinated me. I went to Egypt with my sister Raquel with the Contiki Tour Group for 18-35 year olds. On a dating site in my college years I posted my ideal travel would be a camel ride through the desert of Egypt not knowing it would really become a reality. I just wanted to stand out from the other girls' posts, whose ideal vacation would be drinking tequila on a beach resort.

So, when they say put it out into the universe, they're not kidding. Meanwhile, they fail to tell you that it's a Bible verse, Habakkuk 2:2-3 "Write down the vision and make it plain on tablets so that a herald may run with it. For the revelation awaits an appointed time; it speaks of the end and will not prove

WHAT DESIRE WOULD YOU LIKE TO ACCOMPLISH IN THE NEXT FIVE YEARS? 10 YEARS? DURING RETIREMENT?

false. Though it will linger, wait for it; it will certainly come and will not delay." I didn't even know of this verse's existence in the Bible at the time. Talk about literacy coming alive literally. Remembering these past surreal experiences energizes me with hope for tomorrow. Don't forget to write down your vision. You will reflect back one day and be astounded how easily you checked off your bucket list.

Even if I take the wrong path, I know my God will redirect me in the right direction. I usually take the longer route because I get lost many times. Navigating life was never my greatest asset. That's why I love going hiking and getting lost in the wilderness because I know eventually, I will find my way out.

Once Robert and I hopped on the plane to Hawaii, I discovered his absolute disinterest in travel. I probably booked too many excursions for his liking. Perhaps he preferred just sunbathing by the pool. I call myself, *Dora The Explorer*. I love adventure and

WHAT CARTOON CHARACTER DO YOU MOSTLY RESEMBLE?

breaking out of my regular routine, meeting new people and embracing other cultures. I had assumed that everyone loves to travel and tour. Robert would be content in the same town with the same routine. He acted as if what I planned was a chore, which includes our ceremony. We said our vows on the island of Waikiki.

I arranged for a photographer to pick us up from the hotel and tour us around to capture our pictures in various locations. I also had a videographer to film our personal vows. A Polynesian guy wearing a Hawaiian shirt officiated our marriage but we needed a witness. We grabbed some random jogger passing by for his signature. Our photography tour was four hours long and Robert was growing impatient. He couldn't wait to get out of his suit and back into his normal wardrobe. I was trying to keep cranky pants calm by reassuring him that we would go to a restaurant to eat. I figured he must be hungry. He reminded me of my dad at that moment. My dad usually complains during an event and then brags about all the enjoyable moments after the experience is over. So, I developed tolerance for such behavior.

Robert barely wanted to act excited or be intimate. I was so confused. I waited two years to find out he doesn't even like intimacy. Yet he seemed affectionate in other ways. Sometimes he would display public affection and I would get so embarrassed. Just small gestures of touching my face would make me blush. I just figured, maybe he was struggling with guilt issues with his sister and mother, resulting from his previous past and that's why he is giving me the cold shoulder. I'm not sure. I was trying to make sense out of something completely ambiguous. I had to meditate on the scripture verse Proverbs 3:5, "Trust in the Lord with all your heart and lean not on your own understanding; In all your ways acknowledge him, and he will make your paths straight."

The next day I planned all these excursions. Robert complained relentlessly about getting up at 5am to see the sunrise on a bike tour cycling down the Maui mountain. Then he complained about the long drive down a narrow path while viewing amazing waterfalls. We had seen most of the waterfalls, but I couldn't get him to drive to the very last waterfall up the narrow mountain path. One of the most famous waterfalls of the island. Then he complained about getting up early to get on a helicopter ride viewing a number of volcanic craters and lava. I also added a Pearl Harbor Tour to our agenda. That was probably the only excursion where I didn't hear a peep from him probably since we were grounded. Once we returned to New York he bragged to all his friends about the trip. I thought to myself, *yikes, is he for real?* Talk about disguising his enthusiasm. One of his friends asked if he had seen the most famous waterfall in the area. He had to admit we skipped that one because of his reluctancy.

The first holiday after our marriage, Robert decides to go to Julie's house without me. I told him, "Why should we be separated on our first Christmas? They don't have to like me, but we can be respectful towards one another." Apparently, that was not an option. I felt Robert going there without me was basically him validating their disrespect towards me. I couldn't convince him not to go without me. I figured if I can't go then I'm sending gifts as if I encouraged him to go. The Bible says in Proverbs 25:21-22, "If your enemy is hungry, give him food to eat; if he is thirsty, give him water to drink. In doing this, you will heap burning coals on his head, and the Lord will reward you." So, I decided to sent my husband with cupcakes because they were sweet enough to exclude me. And since I was feeling generous in my Christmas Spirit, I also sent gifts. When Robert returned, he came back with the gifts unopened. I guess the heaping coals on her head didn't allow her to want to open the presents. Or maybe she is just a hot head or a hot mess.

Robert was then invited to attend his niece's communion without me. Here we go again. They were determined to cause more strife in my marriage. Very well, touché. I'm wearing my shield of faith to extinguish all the flaming arrows of the evil one as described in Ephesians 6:16. I wasn't happy about Robert allowing his sister to divide us this way. So, I decided to have Robert deliver my beautiful baguette diamond cross pendant necklace to his niece as her communion gift. I figured if they sent it back, I could wear it myself. Well, Julie has good taste. She kept the necklace and I'm happy my niece was allowed to wear it. Children are always innocent but got caught in the middle of all this drama. But in my heart, I knew her daughter Alexa loved me.

This time Julie sent Robert home with a beautiful Lennox bread tray as a favor gift. I decided to give Julie a call fully aware that she doesn't like me and might not even take my call. "Hi, Julie, it's Ava." Immediately, she hung up. I expected that response. I learned her game quickly. I called back and left a sweet message, "I'm sorry I think we got disconnected, I wanted to share I love the Lennox bread tray favor you sent through Robert." Then I hung up. I was not going to feed her hunger for power by letting her know that her actions affected me or my marriage. But in reality, from the day I said, "I do" my marriage was changed forever- for the worst- with her sly manipulation. Matthew 19:5 says, "For this reason a man will leave his father and mother and be united to his wife, and the two will become one flesh." Becoming one flesh seemed far-fetched when Robert is so emotionally tied to his sister. I've heard of mama's boys but this sibling thing was weird. I don't have any brothers. I never got involved in my sister's relationships to understand these dynamics.

Robert and I attended numerous counseling sessions and private sessions with the pastor of our congregation to help resolve our issues. Everything seemed fine between us except during the holidays when I would be excluded from his family. I waited two years to have my first son Louis. I needed to feel secure in the marriage to bring children into the relationship because we had such a rocky start. While I was in the hospital waiting for my labor pains and contractions, I get a phone call from an ex-boyfriend. "Hi Ava, it's me, Christian." I replied, "Christian who?" I had forgotten all about him. He said, "Are you kidding? You don't remember me?" As I heard his voice my memory rescued me. I replied, "I'm sorry but I'm in the hospital waiting to give birth." Christian replied, "Oh, I'm sorry to disturb you" and we hung up.

Luckily my husband truly believed I didn't know who was calling me. Once I delivered the baby my husband said, "Oh the baby is so cute he looks just like Christian." We just laughed. I enjoyed my husband's dry sense of humor. When everyone left the room, I had a few moments to myself. I called Christian back and I let him know, "I just want to thank you even though we didn't work out together, you helped me build my relationship with Christ."

Christian was the first guy I ever met who knew the Bible inside and out. I had met him at a Halloween event and I was dressed as Santa Clause and he was dressed in a scuba diving gear outfit. He was tall, fit and handsome. How did I meet such a handsome guy dressed as Santa? I'm not sure. I definitely was not attractive wearing a white beard and a red pointy floppy hat. I stuffed a fluffy pillow inside my costume to give me a few extra pounds. When he came to pick me up on our first date, he saw the real me. I'm not sure how he even made a physical connection with me. He probably wanted to know if he was naughty or nice and thought, I was full of spice. Who knows? Turns out he was knowledgeable with scripture and I wasn't. He struck me as super intelligent because he had something I didn't.

I was a Catholic girl and he was a Born-Again Christian who was well-versed in scripture. I desired his knowledge. The problem was I didn't know enough scripture to know if he was sincere in his faith. He took me to my first Christian Church and I saw he didn't even put a dollar in the offering. I wondered, if he is a believer then why wouldn't he give? That struck me as a red flag. A few times his stories did not align with his actions. I thought I would surprise him at his work place and coincidentally (or not), he wasn't working that day. I questioned him about it and he said he wasn't feeling so well so he called in sick.

Another time, I was at the house and it seemed his phone was disconnected. I couldn't put the pieces together but I let him know, something is not right. He then told me, "I have a girlfriend in Puerto Rico that I have been dating for a long time on and off and then I met you and I'm confused and don't know what to do." I said, "I understand now. I'll make it real simple for you. If you choose me, you will always think of her and if you choose her, you will always think of me. So I will decide for you, choose her." I went home and cried my eyes out to God on the edge of my bed.

At the time, my younger sister Raquel and I shared the same bedroom. Sometime after midnight, I had gotten home and crawled into bed after my prayer. My sister Raquel gently put her hands on my back and soothed me to sleep. I felt such warmth and thought to myself, *"how does she know?"* I didn't think anything of it. A few days later, I asked her, "do you remember putting your hands on my back and soothing me to sleep." She immediately said, "No, when was that?" Then I realized that was the presence of the Lord using my sister's physical self. Now I understood this supernatural incredible feeling of warmth and comfort. I was right as well! Years later, Christian would be dating her and contacting me. I'm so glad it wasn't the other way around. God once again validated my decision-making. I'm thankful, Christian piqued my interest to learn the Bible the way he knew it. Even though Christian was a wolf in sheep's clothing, I truly wanted to follow God's teachings. I was already taking Jewish studies at Hofstra University as an elective since I was seeking out the truth.

Robert's sister and mother called me while I was in the hospital to see if they could visit our newborn son Louis. I hadn't spoken to them since the cancellation of the wedding. I immediately welcomed them to visit the baby without hesitation. I didn't even need an apology because I only desired respect from Robert and for him to stand up to me. So, I pretended our marriage was all rainbows and unicorns because I didn't want to give them the satisfaction that they had power over our damaged relationship. His sister and mother continued to pull manipulative stunts to make it look like I was the root of the problem.

I named my second son Jonathan because he is my favorite character in the Bible. Jonathan protects his best friend David against his own father Saul who tries to kill David in 1 Samuel 20. It irritates me when people say, "Blood is thicker than water." If that were the case then David wouldn't run away from his own son Absalom who attempts to kill him in 2 Samuel 15. I just needed my husband to have characteristics of a Jonathan to take my side over his sister. I was going to name my son Jacob but then I learned that Jacob in the Bible stole his brother's birthright in Genesis 27. I didn't want my son to have an association with a name of betrayal. Talk about family dynamics and then people saying blood is thicker than water. I suppose they don't know the scripture Proverbs 18:24 that says, "A man of many companions may come to ruin, but there is a friend who sticks closer than a brother."

When it was time to baptize our son Jonathan, the local church we attended told us that they wouldn't baptize my second son because we had not attended for a few months and our membership had expired. It was the first I heard of something like that. I was so heartbroken. Robert and I used to volunteer with the youth group in this congregation before we had children. I never got a chance to explain why we were not present at the Church for the last few months. I couldn't believe I was kicked out because of my absence. I suppose they didn't have renewal memberships.

Our local church had baptized my first son Louis. It became difficult to attend weekly services because they didn't have a daycare at the time. Bringing my son Louis to church stressed me out, as I did not want to disturb the sermon. The few times I brought Louis, I had to walk out in the lobby area to nurse him and then rush to work afterwards. Now where could I baptize my son? I then decided to go back to the Centerpoint Church where I had gotten baptized. The pastor confirmed that churches do have memberships but their doors are always open to me as a backup church. I was so relieved that we had a relationship where we can pick up where we left off. There is no perfect church but there sure is a perfect God.

Robert was affectionate with the children but never with me. He was not fond of cuddling at night. My husband just acted distant with physical touch. One time, I smacked Robert on the tush out of affection and he said, "You are like a perverted old man!" I thought to myself, *then you must be the cranky housewife*. He wouldn't even allow me to enter the shower with him. I used to get so jealous thinking he was taking long showers and masturbating. Sometimes I would try to peek through the shower curtain to see if I could catch him in the act to try to understand the alienation. I'm sure men can relate to this when wives neglect their spouses once children are conceived. The Bible says in Ephesians 5:25, "Husbands, love your wives, just as Christ loved the church and gave himself up for her. I certainly wasn't feeling this kind of love. Robert couldn't balance loving me and the children.

One night, I was so desperate for affection, I woke Robert up in the middle of the night and we conceived Jonathan. Robert was proud to announce I was pregnant but he didn't know how that occurred. Exactly, what does that mean? Is Robert confessing to everyone that we are not usually intimate? Of course, my sister-in-law jumped to the conclusion that I was with another man. I can't win.

One day, I casually browsed through Robert's Facebook page and saw a selfie of his pectoral muscles and lower abs with his underwear slightly pushed down. I also saw him comment on some girls' Facebook page who looked like a bodybuilder. He was always attracted to women with masculine physiques. One time I found a magazine of female bodybuilders posing on motorcycles tucked underneath the mattress. I questioned him, "What are you trying to attract with these selfies you are posting?" Robert didn't think there was anything wrong with his actions because the Facebook girl was out of state. I said great, "Nothing wrong with that right? Then I'm going to get my bikini and you're going to take pictures of me so I can post online also." Once I was dressed, I handed him the camera and started posing. After our photo shoot I grabbed the camera from him and said, "Are you crazy? Would you allow me to post such pictures? I would never do that! I just wanted to make my point." The next day he told his friend Frankie how he was turned on by me when I put on my bikini and started posing for the camera. Frankie told him, "Your wife is hot and funny. If my wife did that, I would tell her to put her clothes back on." When Robert shared Frankie's feedback I was surprised. I didn't even realize how humorously I handled the situation was. At least someone else appreciated how I was trying to get my point across.

On Mother's Day, I decided to buy Lola a rose gold Michael Kors watch. I even had it delivered to Queens County where she was getting her hair done. I wanted her to enjoy it right away. She seemed very happy with her gift. I decided to buy Lola a gift from the kids as well. I ordered her an origami rose gold necklace with the boys' pendants in the locket. I asked her if she received it in the mail. Her reply was, "Yes, love you." Shortly after I get another text. "Sorry, the text wasn't for you." I was so upset. I told Robert how hurtful that was. He told me to call her and ask her, "Who was the comment for?" I'm not used to confronting people, but that was a great way to approach the situation. That's why I loved Robert because he seemed to know how to handle certain situations. I gave Lola a call and asked her, "I received your text but I was wondering if the text wasn't for me, who was it for?" She replied sternly, "It wasn't for you." Wow, I still didn't know how to respond. Was she just playing a game with me, intentionally looking to hurt me?

Raquel told me boldly, "She doesn't like you and she never will and you need to accept that." Wow. I was finally awakened. She's right. I thought to myself, *"Why do I need her to like me?"* I didn't even realize how much of a people pleaser I was until Raquel told me blatantly and explained, "Some people will just not like you no matter what you do." That made total sense. I needed to accept that hard core truth. I then texted

> DESCRIBE ONE POSITIVE THING ABOUT YOURSELF THAT SOMEONE MAY BE INTIMIDATED BY YOU FOR.

my mother-in-law, "I know you don't like me, but I would appreciate it if you just respect me." I was too much of a chicken to communicate that over the phone because I wouldn't be prepared for the attack response. Most people deflect, use reverse psychology, don't acknowledge their wrongs, justify their actions, and get defensive. I never met anyone that can respond diplomatically when their behaviors are addressed.

I now accept, not everyone is going to like you from the minute they look at you. Sometimes your beauty, intellect, and talents can be intimidating to others.

Sadly, all hell broke loose because I told my mother-in-law how I felt. Julie immediately contacted me yelling, "How dare you talk to my mother that way! She is very ill and she does like you." I told Julie, "I'm very sorry but this is between me and your mother and I would prefer you didn't get involved. Even if your mother is sick, it doesn't give her the right to be disrespectful toward me." I had to then hang up on Julie because people are incomprehensible when they're yelling at you. Now my husband gets wind of the story. He sides with them, ganging up on me. This is exactly why I always avoided confrontation. Here I am, under attack. I can't fight everyone all at once. I'm not allowed to have a voice. Even as a child, I knew it was easier to keep a secret.

CHAPTER THREE

THE LIES I HAD RECORDED IN MY HEAD....

-Why I felt overlooked in life.
-Why I couldn't verbally defend myself.
-Why I needed approval of others.
-Why I would rather give than receive.
-Who truly knew me? I didn't know myself.

The broken record I played over and over in my head was, "I must seek everyone's love and approval, I am not smart enough, I am not pretty enough, and no matter what I do, I will never be good enough." Who will listen and who will believe me? I couldn't find the keys to free me of my shackles. Drama continued to find me even when I tried to avoid it because the roots are connected to the branches. God needs to cut the bad branches, and if we resist this pruning then the wood is only good for campfires to roast marshmallows. John 15 states, "I am the vine; you are the branches. If a man remains in me and I in him, he will bear much fruit; apart from me you can do nothing. If anyone does not remain in me, he is like a branch that is thrown away and withers; such branches are picked up, thrown into the fire and burned."

The branches that needed pruning were the lies from my childhood, my upbringing, and what I learned from my parents, friends, church, and society. Did you know Satan is the father of lies? In John 8:44 says, "He was a murderer from the beginning, not holding to the truth, for there is no truth in him. When he lies, he speaks his native language, for he is a liar and the father of lies." I now tell myself, I am smart. I am perfectly imperfect and beautiful in God's eyes. What broken record have you told yourself? It is time to edit the lyrics and say, "I am noticed by God. I am his masterpiece, created in his image." How do I know? Read Ephesians 2:10 and Genesis 2:26.

Why I felt overlooked in life. I was nominated homecoming queen in high school. How surprising because I wasn't on an athletic team or enrolled in national honors or popular in any way. I tried out for kickline and I didn't make the cuts. I can rehearse all my kicks as if it was yesterday ingrained in my head. I tried out for basketball and again I didn't make the cuts. I just couldn't fit in. Being nominated was a big surprise to me. Not only was I nominated, I was voted as homecoming queen. Of course, I heard rumors that the only reason I won was because the athletic girl Cynthia was absent from school sick. Regardless, I was just ecstatic to have the spotlight on me for just that one moment.

> WE ALL HAVE SPECIAL GIFTS. WHAT ACTIVITY OR TALENT IS YOUR STRENGTH? OR SIMPLY FIND A NEW HOBBY AND KEEP DISCOVERING YOUR BEST SELF.

When I attended my 10-year reunion with Robert they announced the homecoming queen again. To my dismay it wasn't me. For a second, I thought maybe I dreamt it. Is it possible I wasn't the homecoming queen? But there was one person from school who remembered I was overlooked. She approached me and asked, "Weren't you the homecoming queen?" I didn't even know how to reply. I said, "I thought I was." I felt like a groundhog who wanted to retreat to my underground burrow and hibernate until I'm ready to peep my head out enough to show my shadow. These mammals tend to keep to themselves. Hibernation sounded comforting to me at that moment. It was as if the enemy knew my exact triggers and loved poking me with that feeling of being unnoticed as if I didn't even exist. I must have recorded that in my head for so many years that it became my own

> **WHAT TRIGGERS YOU EASILY? RECORD A NEW TRUTH ABOUT YOURSELF.**

truth. But I am now aware of my triggers and I have recorded and meditated a new truth to myself. I'm not set aside, I am set apart, noticed and handpicked by God as his special treasure as I discovered in Deuteronomy 14:2 and so are you!

Why I couldn't I verbally defend myself? I trained myself to be quiet in case I wouldn't be believed. I was molested by a member from a Hispanic society club my parents were involved in. Many times, my parents would have BBQs and salsa dances in the backyard while my god father would try to get me alone inside the house.

I may not have known how to protect myself but I knew how to protect and hide my little sister Raquel in the closet whenever my godfather came over. I would tell Raquel, "Let's play hide and seek." Then my mother would be calling our names, "Raquel and Ava, look who's here, say hello." You would think common sense to wonder, "Why are my children hiding?" If only my mom knew how to read my mind, let alone understand my body language.

The strictness of my upbringing revolved around the mantra of, *Respect your elders. Kids are to be seen not heard.* I wasn't allowed to go to my friends' homes or have friends over, let alone have sleepovers. My mother didn't want to be responsible for other children if anything happened under her supervision. Plus, she kept her house immaculate with her ornate velvet furniture still covered in plastic and glass mirrored walls and victorian lamp shades with a sculpted figurine holding the bulb. The living room was a museum for guests only. Having kids over would unleash a chaotic mess.

Of course, I felt like an outcast from society and lonely at times, but luckily, I had my sisters to play with. If Raquel and I were fighting, my mom would come with the belt and whip us both. She would say, "One of you started and the other finished it, so you're both getting it." She made sure she got her point across. She didn't even want to hear how it transpired. This way there was no picking sides or favoritism. My mother's favorite line was, "This hurts me more than it hurts you." Most of the time we hung out outside with our neighbors and when it was time to come inside my mom would yell from the window, "Come inside!" I didn't have many friends because of the many rules and restrictions my mother had imposed, possibly kept me out of trouble. I heard stories about the people who hung out after school under the bleachers drinking, smoking and whatever else they did.

In middle school, I wasn't allowed to wear make-up. I secretly tried wearing eyeliner to school. I forgot to take it off before I got home. Well, that belt came out quickly. I wasn't even allowed to shave my legs. I felt like a hairy monkey, so I avoided wearing skirts or shorts to gym class. Although my mother raised us very militantly, there was plenty of love with which she compensated. We always had warm home-cooked meals on the stove. My mom provided us with a better lifestyle than she had been raised under. She was born and raised in Puerto Rico on a farm with thirteen brothers and sisters. My mother washed her garments in the river, ate fresh chicken, and drank organic cow's milk from the barn. My mother clothed us in the nicest clothing and showered us with elaborate gifts on the holidays and birthdays. I knew I had a better life than my cousins and neighbors.

Whereas, my oldest sister Silvia compared her life to her classmates' upbringing. My mother didn't do the whole sit-down family dinners after school like Silvia wanted. But there was always a warm pot of food prepared for us after school, waiting on the stove, for us to eat at our leisure. Our sit-down meals were only on Thanksgiving and Christmas without our extended family. Silvia admired families that ritually ate dinner together and celebrated with their relatives on holidays. Fantasizing the greener grass on the other side, she was clueless of the dynamics underlying her friend's families, all of whom had their own battles they were fighting. This only left Silvia discontented with her upbringing and extremely critical of herself, which she projected on us, as if she wished we were never born.

I associated my mother's strictness and assertiveness with being powerful and strong. My father, on the other hand, was funny, playful, social, and very accommodating. I would get away with murder if my mother wasn't around. I felt loved with the structure imposed on all of us by my mother. I didn't always agree with the punishment, such as when I would wet the bed in the middle of the night. When I woke up in the morning in a cozy warm bed, I would realize I wet the bed again. I would dodge under the bed and then my mother would come into my room with the belt, believing it to be the best method to potty train. That was how she was raised. She didn't know any better as none of us had a parenting manual. Thank goodness I had Google to assist me.

I am thankful I was raised with obedience, manners, respect, and I understand the ignorance in my upbringing. I remember Robert used to get infuriated when Louis or Johnathan were wetting the bed. Robert would be tired and cranky and give them a bath in the middle of the night. I would start the laundry and remake the bed with fresh sheets. I had to calm Robert's temper and tell him, "It's ok. I'm here to help you. Don't get upset, it's not a big deal." I didn't understand why Robert would be infuriated, because I knew the boys didn't wet the bed on purpose. I wanted to protect them from the punishments that were done onto me. I didn't even think the yelling was necessary.

The therapist told me I married someone like my mother. I was dumbfounded. I never made the association. Subconsciously, I gravitated to my controlling husband because I was familiar with my mother's personality. Robert was meticulous with a clean home, immaculate like my mother, and authoritative. Perhaps I should have married someone like my father, a people-pleaser. Except, my dad had no boundaries. My father was the "yes dad" unless my mother overruled the

> DO YOU GRAVITATE TO RELATIONSHIPS WITH CHARACTERISTIC SIMILAR TO YOUR MOTHER OR YOUR FATHER? OR NEITHER?

decision. If I told my dad, "Mom did x,y and z to me," he would say, "I understand, but you still have to respect your mother." He always supported my mother's decisions even if he didn't agree. So, I didn't feel as protected by him as I did in my mother's care under her authority. My best memories of my dad were climbing on his toes and being walked around the house. My dad also taught me to ride my first bike. He was always so playful. I used to chase my dad with tears streaming down my face when he would leave to work demanding to go with him.

Why I needed approval of others? I knew my parents loved me, so I didn't need their approval. I looked up to my older sister Silvia as a mentor. She would translate English to Spanish for my parents to guide them because their English was broken. I looked for Silvia's guidance as well. The more she rejected me the more I needed to prove myself to her but failed terribly. Nothing I did was ever good enough. Silvia would correct my pronunciations in a condescending manner. She used to enjoy telling me, "You're so stupid." Being born on her exact birthday didn't help. I liked ice cream and she liked cake. Our personalities were extremely bipolar of one another. I never planned to steal her spotlight each year. She was treated like an adult at a young age because she took that role upon herself. She acted like a mother goose to all of us. Playtime wasn't part of Silvia's recreation.

WHO DO YOU LOOK UP TO AS A MENTOR? WHAT DO YOU ADMIRE MOST ABOUT THEM?

I didn't realize I was overly giving and super accommodating in my friendships for self-approval to compensate for the lack of approval from Silvia. Then, I read a self-help book.

Subconsciously, I was unaware I was transferring my desire of acceptance onto others. The more people affirmed me as a great friend, the more I desired to please them. I enjoyed extending hospitality, help, favors and gifts and in return I would receive affirmation until the scale started to feel unbalanced. I started to feel as if I was being taken advantage of. I felt depleted from giving more of myself and unappreciated. The more I did the more people expected from me. I was always delighted to do for others but they remained unaware of my limitations because I didn't want to disappoint anyone or lose out on friendships by not meeting their expectations.

I told Raquel how it hurts me when Robert comes home and starts wiping down the kitchen counter, when I had left it spotless. She told me, "Ava, why does that bother you? You should be so happy he comes home and cleans the house. You know he is obsessive-compulsive?" She suggested I stop cleaning the house and let him do it. Raquel carried herself like an older sibling and was often the voice of reason. I gave Raquel's question some deep thought that night, *why does it bother me?* I asked God, *She is right, please tell me why it hurts? There is something more to my pain that I need to figure out.* I had to be persistent with God to find out. I truly didn't understand the pain that taunted me each time he cleaned after me. I know I left the house spotless. Three days later I heard the whisper of God. Almost like a light bulb that turned on in my head. *Wow!* I heard, *it wasn't good enough.* This pain had nothing to do with my husband's compulsive cleaning behavior. This is the voice I recorded in my head, "It's not good enough"

This was the subconscious lies of my older sister Silvia's words and behavior towards me, *nothing was good enough.*

Once I had identified my trigger, I no longer took Robert's obsession to clean personally. I began to tell myself a new story, *he cleans after me because it is a learned behavior from his mother.* Perhaps when he is nervous, he starts to wipe things down for comfort or because he finds it therapeutic. Similar to someone who possibly bites their nails, twirls their hair or picks their eyelashes. There is immense freedom in knowing a lie from the truth.

The other lie I told myself was that everyone loved my younger sister more. Seemed as though the attention was mostly directed towards her. She was petite and tiny and you could throw her around. Even as a child, I felt like I was treated more like an

> THINK OF A LIE YOU MIGHT BE TELLING YOURSELF AND TURN IT INTO A POSITIVE TRUTH?

adult just because I was older by two years. You can't really throw me around weighing 100 lbs at ten years old when my sister was half my weight. Food was my friend during elementary school. But I understood life is full of different preferences. I just wasn't one of them. Even now, when I am only 117lbs and 5'1" tall, I sometimes feel like that little pudgy girl who can't lose the five pounds I gained when I was admitted into the mental hospital. I am delightfully surprised when I am told how pretty I look. I usually feel fatter than I look. This is a perfect example that feeling are not facts. Everyday I try to tell myself a new truth.

Why I would rather give than receive? My mother was a giver. She would treat the neighborhood to ice cream when Mr.

Softee truck came around. My mother paid for her sisters to go on a cruise, when my grandmother died. This was my mom's way to compensate them for helping my grandmother when she was ill. My mother was too busy taking care of us. Even when we would go to Puerto Rico to visit family occasionally, my mom was still treating her siblings. I thought we were the guests and they would reciprocate. I suppose they figured my mother was more financially stable than them, so my mother was expected to be generous.

Observing my mother, giving came naturally to me, along with her hospitality. But receiving from others was an uncomfortable feeling. Perhaps because I never saw my mom receiving from others. I felt obligated if I received anything, as if I owed something in return. I don't like having any kind of debts. I also wanted to avoid, if ever, the favor or gift being thrown back in my face. Matthew 6:3 says, "But when you give to the needy, do not let your left hand know what your right hand is doing, so your giving may be in secret. Then your Father, who sees what is done is secret, will reward you." Now I'm happy to say, I'm ready to receive God's very best. I tell myself, "If I don't receive, I block the givers' blessing." Changing my thought process was the key to overcoming the lies.

My other insecurities trailed behind me. Why didn't I like asking for favors? Occasionally I would try asking for small favors. I tried asking a friend, "Can you print something for me?" When an excuse was made explaining why they couldn't help me, I knew not to ask for something bigger. How could I realistically expect a favor when I constantly felt ignored or rejected? One time I asked Virginia for a coupon code on the computer and she couldn't even do that. I knew she was in front of her computer but she acted as though she was busy and continued to stay on the phone talking with me about her personal life. I wasn't surprised. Virginia's personality was so funny. I truly enjoyed her company. Virginia had a gift of making people feel good about themselves, but it came with a price. It came with a self-seeking gratification to overstep her boundaries. One time, I told her, "If you're coming over, please don't park in my father-in-law's parking space," as he was renting the upstairs from us to help supplement our mortgage. What did Virginia do when she came over? Immediately, she parked in the driveway and five minutes later my father-in-law arrived. Pablo was offended that someone was in his parking space. I had to apologize to my father-in-law for my friend's behavior.

Virginia had selective hearing and poor listening skills. She loved to be the center of conversations. Because she was so funny it was entertaining. Her personality was so vibrant, energetic, and she was animated in her storytelling. She was excused from bad behavior, even in her work place. One time, she parked in her boss's VIP guest parking spot and when her boss's wife arrived at the workplace the spot was obviously taken. Virginia would excuse herself with, "I'm sorry, do you want me to move my car?" Knowing that would be more of a hassle. She left people thinking she didn't know better. If the sign says, "Reserved" then she knew she shouldn't park there. When she narrated this story, she left my jaw wide open in amazement.

I once went to the post office with Virginia and she decided to park in the fire zone when there was plenty of parking right, front and center. I never understood her behavior. What I do know is that, if no one tries to tell her otherwise and no consequences were in place, then why would she change her ways? It was probably more fun to break the rules than to follow them. The only thing I could conclude is that she had a controlling grandmother and perhaps she didn't want to be told what to do by anyone, including posted street signs.

Another time, my husband told me I had to tell her to stop calling after 9pm because it's disruptive if the kids are sleeping. I tried to tell her, but it went in one ear and out the other. She still called after hours and thought nothing of it because what she had to share was more important. I needed to feel needed so I enjoyed her calls, and listening to her stories for hours and then feeling like an amazing friend. But eventually I felt burnt out. What was the point of engaging people and their needs, if you're going to be ignored? This was why I couldn't defend myself. It was pointless.

I tried to set boundaries, or at least I thought I did, but I failed terribly. Virginia used to ask for things she didn't even need just to test people's boundaries. She sought more control knowing people-pleasers didn't have limitations. One day she asked me to bring her coffee when I was on my way to deliver her homemade banana pancakes, shrimp penne ala vodka, and spinach salad with strawberries and nuts because she just delivered her first child. This demand made me feel as if I wasn't bringing her enough.

When I arrived at her house, her mother told me, "I don't know why she bothered you for coffee, when she already had one." Virginia cleverly leveraged affirmation to get whatever she wanted in life. I must have had a magnet for controlling friendships and she had a radar for people-pleasers.

When she had her baby shower, I purchased the invitations and thank you cards. I prepared the shower bingo games, purchased party favors and made a three-tier diaper cake for her. When she looked at her registry she asked, "Did you purchase the rocking chair from my registry?" I felt guilty that I fell short of her expectations. I then bought more gifts from her registry. Looking back, I am amazed by how I was manipulated by such an expectant person. I'm so self-aware now, that the drama doesn't follow me anymore. I'm undetectable by the radar. The enemy can't poke at this trigger of mine anymore because I am no longer starving for affirmation. My own words of affirmation to myself are energetic, creative and accomplished.

GIVE YOURSELF THREE POSITIVE ADJECTIVES TO DESCRIBE YOURSELF.

A self-help book I read suggested asking for favors and embracing the response, "No." When the time comes that I am unable to return a favor they too cannot be upset. That made complete sense. I never thought of it that way. It was time to come out of my comfort zone and put what I just learned into practice.

One day, I needed a favor. My children had a birthday party to go to but the bible study I facilitated was at the same time. I asked my Christian neighbor Crystal around the block to take my children to the birthday party and her response was, "I was going to ask you to drive." I suppose that was her way of saying, "No." The book prepared me for this same scenario. Luckily my other girlfriend called me and I told her, "My boys won't be able to attend because I have company arriving soon. Unfortunately, I don't have a ride for them." She immediately came to my house and picked up my boys. Thank you, God for the people who extend themselves without being asked.

A week later, my neighbor Crystal needed a favor from me but I was occupied with something else. I told her I would be able to assist her on a different day. She was used to the old Ava who would reschedule and jump hurdles for others. Crystal looked at me as if I had four eyes. I'm sure she told herself, '*Since when do you say "No"?*' For the first time she looked astonished, rejected and embarrassed. She didn't know how to respond. There was an awkwardness after she left. Finally, I felt honest with myself; I felt authentic. Now this is self-love. Matthew 5:37 says, "All you need to say is simply 'Yes' or 'No'; anything beyond this comes from the evil one." I usually found myself giving an explanation driven by my guilt. Thank you, Lord, for teaching me to keep it simple.

One day, my boys missed the bus and I drove Louis and Jonathan to my neighbors' bus stop. Crystal was standing outside with her son. I asked her, "Can you put Louis and Jonathan on the bus for me?" She looked at me confused as if I spoke a different language. That took me by surprise. Our children attend the same school. I was the one who used to babysit for her so she could have a date night with her husband. Her boys loved my home-cooked meals that I served whenever I babysat them. If anything, I should have been the one staring at her confused.

During my divorce, out of desperation, I needed Crystal to take my children after school. When I picked up my children, they were starving and all she served them was popcorn. I was so upset. I let her know, "I can't believe you couldn't even serve my kids a box of Kraft Mac and Cheese that costs 99 cents. I treated your children like they were my own family!" I used to send her pictures of her two boys eating homemade meatballs and spaghetti, penne alla vodka and buying them dessert from the ice cream truck but she couldn't extend the same courtesy to my kids. She did admit her kids loved me but apparently, she didn't feel the same for my children. These were the ugly truths I didn't want to learn about people. Therefore, it was easier not to ask for favors.

Who truly knew me? I didn't even know myself. When you're a people pleaser, you lose your own identity in the process of serving others. I suppressed most of my pain by being busy. I was a Wig Boutique owner, Realtor, PTA mom, Pampered Chef representative to support a friend while multi-tasking play dates and keeping the house in order. I wore many hats. This behavior or energy in the medical field is considered Manic. I call it being multi-faceted. Did I forget to mention I was a facilitator of my church's *Boundaries* book study, which was held in my home once a week? At night, I go

> WHAT STRATEGY DO YOU USE TO OVERCOME LIFE'S CHALLENGES?

for jogs and journalized before bed. I suppose I had a high octane of energy being fueled by anger. At least I released the energy in a healthy way but it was only a matter of time before I would mentally crash. Being a busy bee was how I numbed my pain.

I remember one time, I cried out to God in my car and I yelled out loud, "God, I had told you I never needed a man in my life. I was happy with my new found relationship with Jesus." I know I said, "If you want to send me a good man as an added bonus, I welcome it." Who knew the result of my request wouldn't allow me to travel? I felt financially strapped. I was able to do more as a single woman. Living life was more fun independently. I downgraded my Volvo Convertible to pay for the home improvements. And when things got tough and I found myself in a tough spot, I didn't know where to pull some extra cash from. My husband didn't earn much. He worked seven days a week while I worked four days. Robert still couldn't contribute as much monetarily. I suppose if his income supplemented the lifestyle I had before, I wouldn't be so disappointed. He was adamant that he couldn't go without his HBO and ESPN, so I couldn't reduce our expenses here. Nor was I able to drop our health insurance which I was paying for through my business. Instead, I went without insurance for a little while to make ends meet and kept his insurance active. I couldn't float both of us financially as well as I could by myself. I truly went into this relationship selfless, making sure Robert was better taken care of than myself.

A week later, Robert called and shared the good news that we won a free cruise to the Bahamas and we only had to incur the port fees. I asked, "How did that happen?" He replied, "When I went to Atlantic City to watch the Ultimate Fighting

> THINK OF A MOMENT WHEN GOD ANSWERED YOUR CRY.

Championship matches at the Tropicana hotel, I filled out a raffle ticket and I was selected as the winner." I told Robert I had just cried my heart out to God about how miserable I was over not being able to travel. I couldn't believe how quickly Jesus heard my complaint and responded with a free Caribbean vacation. At that moment I was reminded of how I bought my house- I lost the bid and I cried out to God. I was so disappointed when Jesus quickly heard my cries and blessed with the house. Wow, I'm such a cry baby. If you are a parent, do your child's tantrums work with you? Our father in heaven loves us the same.

One night, my husband went to Atlantic City to watch the Ultimate Fighting Championship (UFC) without me. It was an overnight trip. I prayed before bedtime and I said, "Lord, I hope my husband is being Christ-like while he is there." Within a half an hour I received a text message, "Peter's girl just grabbed my balls. Where is the after-pool party?" I immediately felt at peace when I received the unexpected text message. I knew the Lord was protecting me. The text was meant for his friend Mario, but came to me, not by accident. I remember telling Robert in the past, "I know you will never cheat on me. Not that I trust you. I trust God to reveal to me if you are disloyal before you do it." I calmly picked up the phone and called Robert, "What after pool party are you going to?" In shock, he replied, "Oh, that was Peter's girlfriend who was drunk!" Calmly I asked, "Okay, Robert can you please come home?" He replied, "I'm not driving three hours to come home at this time of the night!" I said, "You're not! So, you're going straight to your hotel room?" He reassured me he wasn't going to the after-pool party.

I set my alarm for 1am and the Lord blessed me with some peace to take a nap. Otherwise, I would have been a total mental case. I was woken up by my scheduled alarm. I called Robert's hotel room a million times. The operator was annoyed and she told me to try his cell phone instead. I had suspected he wasn't headed to his room following the event. Robert told me the next day he had gone to grab a bite afterwards. Unlikely story, but what was I to do? I knew arguing wasn't going to resolve the situation.

I took my marriage vows seriously before God. I was not leaving till Robert dies or commits adultery. I almost couldn't wait till he cheated in our relationship. I would have had grounds for divorce and I wouldn't have disappointed my sweet Jesus. If I didn't fear God, I probably would have cheated on my spouse because the relationship was rooted in unhappiness. So, I remained faithful. Little did I know, God had devised a different plan for me. Both my business and my marriage were spiraling out of my control. I had exhausted all my resources. I read so many self-help books, joined marriage counseling, went to a Christian marriage retreat, I changed my thought-process, prayed and cried on my knees every night. One day, I read a self-help book that stated, "avoidant and compliant marries controlling." I started to cry. I was completely clueless. If I expressed my desire to eat at a sushi restaurant, he would respond, "I'd rather eat at this steakhouse instead." I would oblige because I didn't read too much into things. I completely overlooked the controlling aspect.

When we went to pick out our kitchen cabinets, my heart was set on the bone color and Roberto picked out the salmon color.

So, I said, "Okay" to his suggestion. When I went to his sister's house and she was remodeling her home, I saw the bone color cabinets being placed in her kitchen. I regretted missing out on that gorgeous, sophisticated look. We needed a saddle between the hallway and the kitchen and I wanted the almond color and he wanted the coral color. You can guess what our saddle was going to look like. I was very compliant. I felt God had my best interests at heart when I received a phone call that the saddle was cracked and if I was okay with the almond color instead. Finally, I got something I wanted. I didn't want to be that girl "avoidant and compliant" any longer.

Once I began setting boundaries in my life, my greatest fears materialized. I had to face the change of circumstances. Everyone perceived me as insane for speaking up. Perhaps if I was always confrontational, I would have been considered normal. The change that I brought about in my life led to the loss of my husband, my children, and my house, because I escaped, unwilling to be coerced into taking medication. I was diagnosed with bipolar disorder. Again I was not believed and misunderstood. Depression wasn't my real symptom. My broken heart was my illness. I had to remind myself through all this that I'm not alone. God is with me. Even though I'm about to enter the world as a single mom, I have a Father in Heaven who loves me and will fight my battles. I eloped from the mental hospital with the whisper of God's voice. Elijiah the prophet heard God's gentle whisper in 1 Kings 19:12, after the powerful wind, earthquake, and fire.

I remember our marriage counselor Fay told me, "Another woman would be happy with your husband." I couldn't believe the audacity. I thought to myself, *well, there are only two women in this room right now.* I didn't know how to respond to that since I was non-confrontational. During my next visit to my therapist office, I rehearsed what I would say with my younger sister. I let Fay know, "I didn't appreciate that comment you made last week because we should be discussing my issues, not another woman's preferences." Fay is married to the pastor of the church my husband used to attend. On another occasion, she shared that she was thinking of my husband when she was at her annual doctor's visit. Fay continued to explain, "I saw dog hair on my jacket and thought how I had to find my lint brush." I thought, *why would you have him on your mind?* She must have been attracted to him. He was the quintessential man for most women. He doesn't like sex, he cooks like a chef, and he keeps the house immaculate because he is obsessive-compulsive. She probably wanted a housewife for herself or a Gay husband. That is how I felt married to Robert.

A book entitled, "Why I don't like Sex" was displayed at a Christian retreat I attended with my husband. I brought it to Fay's attention because it did not seem like an appropriate book to rekindle your marriage. In 1 Corinthians 7:5-15 says, "Do not deny yourselves to each other, unless you first agree to do so for a while in order to spend your time in prayer; but then resume normal marital relations." I lost count of how many times I was denied lovemaking. Fay seemed intrigued and even interested in the book. She noted down the name of the book for herself. She proceeded to say, "I don't want it for myself, just for a client of mine." I thought that was a half truth. She seemed to be put off by sex too. Fay had many characteristics similar to Robert in many ways, so she related more to him and did not believe he had any underlying issues.

Since I was sexually molested as a child, she said, "According to my research, statistically, women who have been molested don't desire to engage in intercourse with their spouse." She was surprised I did not fall into that category. She was aware that oftentimes, I would suggest to Robert, "Can you transfer the children from my bed once they fall asleep so we could be together?" I would wake up the next morning sexually frustrated. Both Jonathan and Louis would still be in my bed. Fay told me, "Consider quality time as the whole family." I told her, "We do that on a regular basis. I believe quality time is one-on-one interaction. I think it's equally important to do this with the children as well." I was becoming painfully aware of the fact that our perspectives were clashing and each session was hindering the progress I was seeking.

I have learned over the years most people speak in relation to their own circumstances and contexts, while referencing your scenarios. I could only assume that she was molested and thus, couldn't relate to my desire for alone time and intimacy. I probably learned more about her than she learned about me.

Our first meeting with Fay required us to fill out a bubble sheet assessment to learn more about our personality traits. She disregarded Robert's analysis outcome, where controlling was emphasized in dark gray. She only wanted to focus on my analysis outcome, where anxiety and passivity were circled in dark gray. Fay revealed that her scores were high for controlling as well. It was evident she didn't want to reflect on Robert's controlling characteristics because she was evasive with that topic when it concerned my husband too. After these three incidents, I discontinued our counseling sessions.

What I did obtain from our sessions were worksheets on how to better communicate during unfair fights, such as bringing up the past and deflecting. It is recommended to discuss a particular topic within 48 hours before moving on. The worksheets also explored how to avoid

> HOW OFTEN DO YOU REITERATE WHAT SOMEONE SAID, TO MAKE SURE YOU UNDERSTOOD THEM CORRECTLY?

closed ended questions leaving me with a single word answer such as "yes," "no" or no response at all. I had to lead my conversations with open ended questions instead, such as, "What did you hear me say?" In order to make sure I was heard correctly. I learned how to avoid trigger words, such as "you make me feel." Instead, I learned to say, "I feel x, y and z when x, y, and z." I also learned about validating people first so they know they are heard and then sharing my own feelings in a non-defensive tactic. We often assume we understand people's intentions, especially if there are underlying implications. Who knew the English language was so intricate.

Robert had a charm about him that women would tell me how lucky I was to have a husband that cooked so well. I wanted to say, "Wow, you don't work and you expect to be served also. How nice would that be, not to work and have a meal waiting for you after a long day of shopping on Amazon." I used to cook for my husband, but he never seemed interested in what I prepared. I had the BlueApron meal kit delivered to my home to impress Robert with gourmet recipes. I thought food was the way to a man's heart. His excuses were, "I ate already. I'm not hungry now. I'll have it tomorrow or I forgot to bring it to work." So, in the refrigerator it remained. There was no turning him on.

We used to have elaborate birthday parties at our home and Robert would prepare five trays of food. He was known for his Seafood Paella, famous Meatballs, Chicken Parmesan, Penne Alla Vodka, Sausage and Peppers. We would also hire an attendant to grill on the BBQ. I prepared a decorative fruit salad and placed a flower garnish as the final touch. I added intricate details for the luau theme and prepared the salad. I staged the home with restaurant-grade linens and added my magic touches. Everyone raved about my strawberry spinach salad with pistachios and mozzarella balls. Robert was so disappointed that the focus was not on his five trays of food. He was so disheartened, he brought it to my attention. I realized he didn't want me to outshine him. He wanted me to stick to baking, since he was not as talented in that arena. It was discouraging that he needed all the affirmation for himself as if we were competing. Didn't he know this was a team effort?

My situation at home was getting worse. I told Robert how I was disappointed with the last birthday party we hosted. Robert allowed the dog to be around the guests, despite my complaint that many people were scared of dogs, especially pitbulls, including his mother and sister. I just wanted all my guests to feel comfortable. I used to be scared of dogs myself and I understand the discomfort of being around animals.

I was attacked by two dogs when I was young. My grandmother's dog Charlie and my aunt's dog Blackie attacked me when I was minding my own business. Dogs sense when people fear them and are more prone to attack. I told Robert that it would best to keep our dog inside to avoid the situation of adults teasing the dog and getting her rambunctious. This has happened before and the dog ran around the yard full speed and could have tripped someone. He agreed to accommodate my request until the day of the event. I waited a few days to address the situation. I started to cry because I was tired of being heard and ignored. Robert looked at me with no remorse, nor verbal response. My dog began to cry at this moment. I got on my knees and hugged Scooby because I knew she felt my pain. At least someone understood me. She was such a well-mannered obedient dog. It was then that I understood why some people love animals more than people.

I don't remember what transpired after our conversation but Robert struck my face and I hit him back. My impulsive reaction was to demonstrate that I wont be intimidated by him. This was the first time he displayed physical abuse. I ran out the front door as fast as a bullet so the situation wouldn't escalate. I quickly got in my car and drove to my parent's house. I filed a police report once I reached their home.

Robert quickly showed up at their house explaining his story to the cops first, while still outside. Robert accused me of hitting him. The police explained that when two adults blame each other, both parents will be taken into custody, leaving the child all alone. That sounded like a tangled web we had haphazardly weaved. If you call the cops, you run the risk of being arrested over false charges. If you don't call, the hitting persists and only gets worse with time.

The next day, I went to my local precinct to file a report. The officer redirected me to the Family Court. When I pulled into the parking lot of the Family Court, Robert was right behind me. I thought to myself, *what was going on? How did he know I was coming here?* I then remembered that my Bible study leader Julio had called me in the morning and I told him what was happening. Julio tried to talk me out of filing a police report and he prayed with me. He must have spoken with Robert after our conversation. How else would Robert have known to find me at the Family Court? Why didn't I learn from my childhood? This is why secrets are imperative. People like to get involved in my life and make things worse. They think they're helping you. I immediately exited the parking lot.

Robert tried to apologize but I wasn't ready to forgive him right away. When I finally got over my pain, I invited him out for dinner like he had previously suggested. He said, "No, not right now I'm watching the UFC." I knew then, he truly wasn't sorry. I got so frustrated. I slipped on a sexy tight black dress. I put my stilettos and clipped in my hair extensions. I applied lip gloss, fake lashes and left. I said, "Enjoy your UFC" as I shut the door behind me. I didn't tell him where I was going. Once I got in the car I said, *God where am I going? I'm not looking for anyone else in my life. I just want to be noticed by my spouse.* I heard God's whisper, "Go to your babysitter's house and ask if she wants to go to the movies with you." She was delighted to go with me. I asked, "Can I borrow a pair of slippers?" I then took my high heels off and my hair extensions out and enjoyed the movie.

I got home at midnight. Finally, I got Robert's attention because he immediately seduced me when I arrived past midnight. We had the most amazing sex. He never asked, "Where did you go?" I thought to myself, *wow, is that all it took to be noticed?* I'm sure God heard my prayers. I said, "Thank you Lord! Robert surprised me physically and ravished me when I got home." At least someone is listening to me. After all, in 1 Corinthians 7:3-5 says, "The husband should fulfill his marital duty to his wife, and likewise the wife to her husband. The wife's body does not belong to her alone but also to her husband. In the same way, the husband's body does not belong to him alone but also to his wife. Do not deprive each other except by mutual consent for a time, so that you may devote yourselves to prayer. Then come together again so that Satan will not tempt you because of your lack of self-control."

I sent my cousin Isabelle an email that read, "I will not be submissive to a man that bullies me and threatens me. You have no idea what is going on. When I told you I attempted to file a police report against Robert because he hit me, you were in denial. You told me he is not capable of doing that. So, again, you called me a liar indirectly and dismissed my pain. Someone who loves me, believes me. I was just at Family Court to get an order of protection. My marriage is getting ugly. I am sorry once again if you are in disbelief. I am sorry I will not be able to attend your

Halloween party. Please don't respond to this email as I am hurting right now and would appreciate my space. If you love me, you will respect my wishes."

CHAPTER FOUR

MY MARRIAGE IS CRUMBLING AFTER A DECADE AND SO IS MY BUSINESS. IS IT TIME TO DIVORCE MY WIG STORE? HOW DO I REINVENT MYSELF?

When it rains, it pours. Wig Boutique blessed me with fifteen years of consistent success, but eventually, financial instability began to consume it. It came down to me sending the building manager my one month notice and I was all set to close Wig Boutique. I never imagined dissolving my business. I felt like I was going through two painful divorces. I was invested wholeheartedly in my career for over a decade. It was therapeutic for me to use my artistic gift to style my customers as if they were my blank canvas and the wig was the final magnificent touch to their wardrobe. Because I loved my job, I felt married to the store. Many times, I was amazed with the glamorous transformation my clients experienced as if ready for a modeling shoot. I felt like a celebrity makeup artist. Building customers self-esteem was my reward.

Life as I once knew it was all coming to an end. I felt so broken. Perhaps a new location would ignite a new zeal and romance within me. The stale repetitiveness of my everyday routines meant that I had to reignite my fire. I consistently strive to

> WHAT NEW DISCOVERY CAN YOU LEARN ABOUT YOURSELF, YOUR MARRIAGE, RELATIONSHIPS WITH OTHERS, OR YOUR WORKPLACE? WHAT MAKES YOU FEEL PURPOSEFUL IN LIFE?

reinvent who I am to grow and avoid boredom. How can I find new passion in my business to feel stimulated again? What will my purpose-driven life look like moving forward? I will have to ponder these questions.

My life became an adventure when I was put in a psychiatric facility against my will just three days later. Thankfully, I had stored away all my merchandise in my garage. The manager was threatening to remove my stuff immediately. I was forced to close my Wig Boutique on Halloween during work hours. This was absurd. I planned to remove my merchandise after ceasing operations the next day. Moving my showcase counters and massive inventory while my customers were still present at the store was such a hazard and unprofessional. I was always punctual with my rents. I was very accommodating when they asked me to move my concession a million times. Meanwhile, the other vendors who were difficult retained their spots. I never liked confrontation.

I suppose I was easy to boss around. I couldn't believe how I was being bullied. I called my husband crying, while explaining how I was being treated. He didn't come to help me or even offer any words of comfort. Robert was too busy trying to get ready to go to my cousin Isabelle's Halloween party with Louis and Jonathan. I didn't allow my children to celebrate Halloween 'trick or treating.' If they wanted to dress up, it couldn't be offensive or spooky. Instead, we would go to the church and celebrate the harvest by carving out pumpkins, face painting, cupcake decorating, and playing in the inflatable bounce houses. My husband decided to go against my wishes and take the boys at night to get some Halloween treats. Our values were certainly different.

I told the manager with tears streaming down my face, "Not only is my business suffering but my marriage is too. I have no one to help me move my stuff. You can just throw out everything from my store." She was shocked. The manager saw me as the girl with the perfect life because of my cheerful spirit. No one was aware of the pain behind my smile. My marriage was sacred. Talking badly about my husband would only be an ugly reflection of myself. I didn't mind telling people about my evil in-laws because they are not a reflection of me.

Once she understood my life was imperfect just like everyone else's she felt sympathy and a deeper connection with me. She told me, "The booth is not rented. You don't have to rush to get your merchandise out." My father heard about management forcing me out the same day. Immediately, my dad and brother-in-law showed up at the store and started packing everything in a truck. I kept telling my dad, "No! No! Robert is coming, he will help me tomorrow. The manager gave me more time to move." My dad wouldn't hear it. I wanted to believe my husband was coming to help me move.

My friend Erica whom I had just become acquainted with dropped by at Wig Boutique. She too began helping me move all my merchandise out of the store. Not too long ago she was forced out of her teaching career. I had helped her move all of her belongings out of her classroom with no assistance. She too was bullied out of the school and was told she couldn't enter the building once unemployed. When I arrived at the school to get her belongings, maintenance was forbidden from helping me. My Honda Pilot was able to transfer all her belongings in one trip. How bizarre, Erica unexpectedly was reciprocating the favor. When strangers witnessed what was happening, they too began to help me move. Once I arrived at my house and unpacked the car, I put my arms around my dad like a little girl and broke down crying. For the first time in my life, I felt my Dad's protective spirit. I almost didn't want to let go. My childhood years didn't allow me to feel safe. Secrets were easier to handle than not being heard or believed.

My wig store was officially closed on an evil holiday. Everyone's lawn was decorated with creepy morbid dead dolls. I never understood why people enjoyed celebrating the mutilated dead just for candy. Harvest fall decor graced my front lawn with pumpkins, corn stock pillars and mums. But that didn't stop my house from being haunted. Sounds insane, unless you're into creepy movies. What can I tell you? Seven or more evil spirits must have visited my home.

I remember when Robert and I had gone to see Fay, our Christian Therapist, she told Robert, "When a follower of Christ backslides meaning, goes back to his old ways, you bring evil spirits to your home." She made us refer to Luke 11:24 and Mathew 12:43-45 which explains, "When an evil spirit comes out of a man, it goes through arid places seeking rest and does not find it." Then it says, "I will return to the house it left. When it arrives, it finds the house swept clean and put in order. Then it goes and takes seven other spirits more wicked than itself, and ey go in and live there. And the final condition of that man is worse than the first." It's possible my husband welcomed those seven spirits into our home because my house looked exactly like this verse from the Bible.

My home was always swept clean and in order. Robert wouldn't have it any other way. I felt I brushed many of our circumstances under the carpet. I was unaware of this spiritual warfare unravelling in the unseen world that tries to combat us. I learned in 1 Peter 5:8, "Be self-controlled and alert. Your enemy the devil prowls around like a roaring lion looking for someone to devour. Resist him, standing firm in the faith, because you know that your brothers throughout the world are undergoing the same kind of suffering." My brain was not shutting down to get some well-deserved rest because I was being attacked from so many different angles.

Who did I marry? I asked myself. After we returned from our honeymoon, my spouse refused to step foot in church. Meanwhile, that was where we first met. Nor did he want to continue helping others recover from drugs and alcohol. I didn't realize how imperative staying connected in sobriety was until the counselor pointed it out to Robert. Robert's love for Christ and helping others were the main ingredients to winning my heart. A converted bad boy was appealing to me also. I thought I married a fearless Christian man. I figured he worked out all his demons before the start of our relationship leaving room for growth. I couldn't have been more wrong. I thought to myself, *Is this the same man who prays beautifully and has scripture verses memorized?* Therefore, I needed to get to Punta Cana Paradisus to chat with God and figure out some unanswered questions? This seemed like the perfect place for some rest and closure. Let's not forget my spa treatments.

Upon closing my store, my steady customers came in to purchase two or three wigs at a time, just in case. I had earned almost $10,000 after I announced that I would be relocating. This was the first time in 15 years I dipped in my savings account to keep the store open. I definitely didn't want to deplete that account and fall short on my other monthly payments. I didn't know my new location was going to be an inpatient facility three days later. God gave me exactly what I needed to survive my adventure. Not one friend of mine offered shelter to me when I couldn't return to my parents' house afraid that they would put me back in the hospital.

I was unemployed and homeless. My funds were running low. I went to the Department of Social Services to apply for a temporary assistance program called SNAP for Food Stamps. As I was waiting for hours for my interview, a guy who was applying for rental assistance asked me my name. I'm thinking, *Oh great! Is this what my life has come to? Broke dating broke.* He then proceeded to say, "I would like to see you again. Can I have your phone number?" *How do I get out of this one?* I'm not good with hurting people's feelings, so he got my 10 digits. I made sure his calls went straight into voicemail. I was better at avoiding situations than addressing the hard truth, "I'm not interested."

CHAPTER FIVE

FALSELY ACCUSED SUICIDE ATTEMPT AFTER A MINOR CAR ACCIDENT. WHAT'S NEXT, A STRAIT-JACKET?

I closed my eyes and when I woke up, I felt confused as if I was still dreaming or acting in a movie set. I was just waiting for the producer to say, "Now cut, lights, camera, action." My reality felt so surreal. I woke up in a different bedroom. I was strapped down to a bed, against my own will institutionalized in a psychiatric ward. *What's next, a strait-jacket?* Now how does that happen? Exactly, only in *A Nightmare on Elm Street* movie. I kept mentally sane believing I was filming a movie instead of feeling trapped in this horrific dream.

Let me tell you what happened. I was driving to Stamford, CT to get my passport because I lacked the energy to power through the crowds in NYC. On my way home, I had gotten into a no-fault car accident. The other driver must have been in my blind spot speeding when I switched lanes. The collision was lightning quick. The police appeared at the scene in seconds.

I immediately called Robert to tell him what happened. Robert told me, "Go to the hospital to make sure you're alright." I told him I was on my way to the high school to vote in the 2015 United States midterm election. Sorry, I can't tell you who I voted for, so you can continue to enjoy my story. I got my ballet in before going to the hospital. It was my first vote ever because I was still learning the politics of life in so many different arenas. I then received a phone call from Carolina's husband Paul. He doesn't normally call me. He was calling to see if I was okay. Perhaps my husband called him. How else would Paul have known I was in a small car accident? I slightly stuttered when I began to tell Paul I was at the high school voting. Paul asked me, "Do you want me to pick you up and take you to the hospital?" I thought about it for a second because I found the stutter a little odd. So, I waited for Paul to arrive.

Within 15 minutes Paul came and I hopped into his car. Paul told me, "Wait inside the car, so I can check to see if there is a long wait in the emergency room." I didn't think anything of it until Paul returned and told me to come inside and the nurse asked me, "Are you wanting to commit suicide?" I replied, "Suicide?" Her response was, "Yes, Suicide." I told her, "I was in a small car accident but I was not attempting suicide." I was so confused. The nurse asked me, "Is Paul your husband?" I told her, "No!" She told me, "He said, you wanted to commit suicide." I wasn't sure why he would do that.

I was asked to wait for the doctors to see me. The hospital held me for a very long time. It was almost midnight. I'm being interrogated with a million questions. "Why were you getting a passport? Where were you planning to travel? How come you were going by yourself? Who was going to take care of your children?" And the interrogation continued. I couldn't believe I was explaining myself as if I needed permission to travel. I'm independent and I used to travel alone many times while single. When I had my second son, I traveled to Puerto Rico to escape and rejuvenate. It's unfortunate more women don't know how to enjoy their own company.

Most women experience postpartum depression because of sleep deprivation. Your brain can malfunction when drowsy. The ability to maintain memory, attention and focus lessen. Lack of sleep can lead to a poor immune system. Your metabolism is slower

> RECOMMENDED SLEEP SHOULD BE 7-9 HOURS. HOW MANY HOURS DO YOU SLEEP?

when you are sleep deprived, which leads to weight gain. Poor cognitive ability is a recipe for disaster. Most women could use more rest to avoid many unhealthy ailments. Exercise, therapy, journaling and eating healthy is self-care to relieve stress and help balance life. Sugar plays a role in your mood swings as well. Don't allow foods to sabotage your happiness and well-being. You can find yourself feeling tired after overindulging.

Most of the time, I found myself putting others before myself. I was neglecting my own needs, which can cause mental breakdowns. If you don't take care of yourself, your brain can get short circuited. Which is what happened to me because my brain would not shut off to recharge itself.

Paul was still in the hospital making sure they don't discharge me. I heard Paul saying, "You're not going to Punta Cana to marry Jesus." Perhaps he doesn't understand Isaiah 54:5 says, "For the Maker is your husband - the Lord Almighty is his name." What's wrong with thinking you want to be the bride of Christ? Yeah, that would sound absurd to marry Jesus. But when I was booking my accommodations to the Punta Cana Paradisus Palma Real Golf & Spa, all inclusive, the lady at the resort had a slight accent and she kept saying, "Para Jesus" not Paradisus. I said to myself, *Wow, is she literally telling me I'm going for Jesus?* with a Spanish accent. The story got even weirder. So, I made the reservations thinking, *Okay Jesus I'll meet you there and we need to talk because the guy I thought I married isn't really the same guy I eloped with. You need to explain this to me.* That is why I was planning my trip alone to meet with Jesus. I had a few pampering spa treatments included in my itinerary. My friends thought I was out of my mind because how can I possibly marry Jesus? Or perhaps they were jealous I was vacationing on my own. I just wanted a romantic getaway with my sweet Jesus. What better place than a resort called Paradisus, like paradise? So I probably spoke in metaphors. Jesus speaks in parables. I remember my son Louis saying to me, "Mom God is Omnipresent." Okay I admit my brain was sleep deprived triggering symptoms of bipolar disorder.

Finally, I was able to make a phone call from the local hospital. Instead of calling a lawyer, I called my accountant to inform him that I was at a hospital and they were keeping me there. My accountant Roger told me, "You can just walk out." But apparently, it wasn't that easy. I was hoping Roger would come to my rescue. Most likely he didn't want to mix business and personal relationships. My accountant knew my marriage was in despair. Roger had provided me with the contact information of the lawyer who was handling his divorce. I had met with the attorney a day before my car accident. "Oh boy" was she a Pitbull. She was probably 4'11" and super assertive. She hardly let me speak. She was quick with her mouth and sharp with her tongue. I was being charged $500 an hour. I searched for less expensive representation but they all asked who was my current attorney. All of them responded, "Wow, you have her representing you! She doesn't lose many cases."

Now I understand the phrase, "It's cheaper to stay married." *Why couldn't I marry a guy like my attorney?* I thought to myself. I felt safe with her to fight my battles. If only I knew how to defend myself. I probably wouldn't be in this predicament. But ouch! $500 an hour. How could I ever afford this? I only make $500 gross a week. I told the Lord, *"Please fill my jars of oil like you did for the widow."* The creditors were going to take her two children as slaves for her unpaid debts." In the scripture 2 Kings 4:2-7, Elisha said to the widow, "What can I do for you? Tell me, what do you have in the house?" And she said, "Your woman servant has nothing in the house except a jar of oil." Then he said, "Go around and get jars from all your neighbors. Get empty jars, many of them. Then go in and shut the door behind you and your sons. Pour the oil into all these jars, and set aside each one that is full.*"* So she went from him and shut the door behind her and her sons. They took the jars to her, and she kept pouring. When the jars were full, she said to her son, "Bring me another jar." And he said to her, "There is not one jar left." Then the oil stopped flowing. She came and told the man of God. And he said, "Go and sell the oil and pay what you owe. You and your sons can live on the rest." What stood out to me the most in this story was that Elisha specifically told her not to ask for just a few jars, many jars. Sometimes in life we shouldn't limit the abundance that God has in store for us. The widow was able to pay off her debt and obtained extra money to live and so will I.

Where there is a will, there is a way. Especially when you walk with the Holy Spirit. My attorney sought a retainer of $2,000 because I was just looking for a post prenuptial agreement. I had purchased my home before marriage. Robert's name wasn't on the deed, it was only on the mortgage note. Technically, he wasn't entitled to the home legally. I didn't know this. Did I really think my husband would sign a post prenuptial agreement? It was basically my plea to say, "Please stop the games so we don't end up in a divorce." But looking back, how unrealistic I was. I wouldn't have signed it if I were him either. So, this lawyer just robbed me of my money because what man in his right mind would agree to this?

My attorney's office was in the 666 building. Of course, that was a red flag but her reputation sold me and I was desperate. Her personality was fearless. I already felt like I was in the furnace in her office. I just

> THINK OF A MOMENT WHEN YOU WERE PENNILESS AND GOD STILL PROVIDED.

remembered Daniel 3:17, Our God whom we serve is able to deliver us from the burning fiery furnace. So, I took my chances. I thought to myself, *sometimes you have to play fire with fire.* I really needed a fire extinguisher with holy water to expunge the flames.

My ex-husband knew I had visited this attorney and he devised this clever plan to have me admitted. How strategic to paint my car accident as a suicide attempt. My vehicle was still drivable. My girlfriend Carolina, who I believed was my friend, was a social worker. Her husband, who drove me to the hospital knew how to have me admitted because she deals with patients of mental disorders on a daily basis. Talk about having friends that are sheep in wolf's clothing. I never imagined my husband would have a wolf pack.

The story gets better. This is some plot that you see in the movies and never expect it to end up being your reality. I felt like Joseph in the Bible where his brothers plotted to kill him in Genesis 37:19, "Here comes the dreamer! They said to each other. Come now, let's kill him into the cistern and say that a ferocious animal devoured him. Then we'll see what comes of his dreams." Here's my warning to you readers, be careful who you disclose your dreams to. Did you know that Luke 21:16 says, "You will be betrayed even by parents, brothers and sisters, relatives and friends, and they will put some of you to death. Everyone will hate you because of me." I had felt so betrayed by my spouse, friends and family, just like this scripture. Joseph brothers intended to harm him, but God used those circumstance for good. I trust what I'm going through is painful, but I wait in anticipation to see the final outcome of God's greater purpose with victory.

Now let me be completely honest with you, I told a few friends I was going to Punta Cana to marry Jesus. I didn't mean it literally. My brain was sleep deprived from functioning on three to four hours of sleep for a few days now. I anchored onto Jesus and sounded a bit fanatical. Fanatical people scare me too. Did you know sleep deprivation leads to delusions, hallucinations, and paranoia? In the same way, patients who stay awake for 24 hours tend to experience symptoms of schizophrenia. So what's wrong with going to an island to rest without two children, meddling in-laws and a spouse that works 7 days a week and gets home at 7pm? I was usually in bed by 9pm because I was running on empty. Sleep deprivation triggered Bipolar and hijacked my mind.

I admit I couldn't speak properly, but it was beyond my control. I remember everything I said that would scare me also. What I really meant to say was, "I wanted to go to Paradisus Punta Cana where I was supposed to originally marry Robert. I needed to spend time with God alone and figure out, who did I get on the plane with to elope?" The day I said, "I do," he didn't want to be intimate with me. I was celibate for two years until marriage, only to then be rejected from sex. Robert also never wanted to step foot in a church again. On Sundays, Robert would check-in the children at the church daycare and then tell me he had to go to work. He couldn't stay for the sermon.

One day, Jonathan wasn't feeling well and I left in the middle of the service to find Robert walking the dogs when I arrived home. This must have been his idea of working. One disappointment after another were lined up like a domino effect. There was nothing I could do. I felt helpless. I married a make-believer who had tattooed an Eagle with a scripture verse that read, Isaiah 40:31, "But those who hope in the Lord will renew their strength; they will fly up on wings like eagles; they will run and not be tired; they will walk and not be weary." I didn't realize that verse was really for me to memorize. I had to fly like an eagle.

Did you know eagles are solitary birds? They are independent and they only fly with other eagles, not sparrows or ravens or other small birds. Eagles have far vision. So, I'm learning to be like an eagle. I want to create and materialize bigger visions for my life. That's why I'm writing this book. Eagles are fearless. I will not allow failure to scare me. Failure is the foundation to valuable lessons that strengthen us. The most fascinating thing I learned about an eagle is they make love in the air. Sounds exotic to me, especially because I was sexually deprived from my spouse. The eagle tattooed on Robert's arm covered up the Tasmanian Devil he previously had on his upper bicep. What cartoon character do you resemble? I like to describe myself as Dora the Explorer. Perhaps that expression is true when they say, "a tiger never changes his stripes."

I like to describe myself as an Eagle. Eagles soar above the rain clouds and use the fierce winds to glide while they lock their wings and easily soar. I can't wait to go kite-gliding so I can literally feel like I'm sailing through the winds

DID YOU KNOW EAGLES ARE THE ONLY BIRDS THAT LOVE STORMS? WHAT ANIMAL WOULD YOU DESCRIBE YOURSELF AS?

like an eagle. I want to go out of my comfort zone and step out of faith to go sky diving because sometimes in my life I just want to jump out of a plane, knowing God will land me safely because he loves me. I want to be fearless above the storm and on solid ground. I can't wait to see how you, Lord, plan to finish the chapters of my life.

As a result of escaping from the mental hospital, my spouse managed to get an order of protection against me. I couldn't go back home as he also changed the locks on the door. I didn't even know the phrase eloping a mental hospital meant escaping. So, I suppose I eloped three times. I escaped to Hawaii to get married, I escaped my marriage, and escaped a mental facility.

Once I discovered Robert evicted me from our home, I served him divorce papers. This is total abandonment and grounds for divorce in the Catholic faith. While in court Robert told me, "I don't want to get divorced, but you still can't look through my phone." I'm still unsure what he planned to achieve with that statement. He stated that I'm not allowed to look at his text messages with his sister or mother. I told him, "I don't care if it's your mother, sister, or another woman texting you. Whatever you are hiding is obviously worth losing your marriage over." Any man can easily put another woman's name under a different alias. I told him, "Beware of sharing personal things about us to your sister or mother. In the Bible, even Miriam and Aaron were rebuked for talking against Moses' wife in Numbers 12. This angered God because Moses was the most humble man more than anyone on the face of the earth. Miriam, Moses's sister, ended up with Leprosy which are skin lesions where the flesh was eaten away. This was her repercussion for gossiping toward God's faithful servant Moses' wife. Luckily Moses asked God to please heal his sister Miriam. God heard Moses' plea and only confined Miriam outside the camp for seven days. I hope my husband's family was not texting ill of me because God will hold them accountable one day. I hope they don't get Leprosy.

The judge ordered we *co-nest* until the divorce is settled. I never heard this term before. This means the kids reside in the family home while the parents take turns moving in and out of the house. This allows the children to have less disruption in their lives.

CHAPTER SIX

ELOPED THE MENTAL HOSPITAL AND CHASED BY COPS, AS IF I COMMITTED A CRIME.

You're probably asking yourself, *how do you elope a mental hospital?* They have padlocks and tight security throughout the entire building. At first, I tried calling my Empire United HealthCare to drop my insurance so I can be released. I thought, no money, no service. The next day, the doctors were ready to release me after my insurance was dropped. This was a genius plan, until the hospital informed my parents I was not covered. My mother reinstated my health insurance by making a payment. My plan was *almost* fool-proof. I was still admitted against my will. God had a better plan for my escape. I believe I had my guardian angels with me. The word angel comes from the Greek word aggelos which means messenger. Angels exist but I don't pray to them. The book Revelations 22:8-9, reveals John bowing down before the angel to worship him. The angel quickly reprimanded John, "Don't do that! I am a fellow servant with you and with your brothers the prophets and of all who keep the words of this book. Worship God!" In the book Matthew 4:9 also clearly states, "Worship the Lord your God, and serve him only."

It was that simple to walk out. I was being transferred to the court house because I refused medication for my manic bipolar diagnosis. The taxi driver that was transporting the patients to the court house said he wouldn't leave without me. Apparently, the nurses tried to have me miss my departure. They told me my transportation was delayed. The nurses also insisted I leave wearing my gown over my clothing. This would alert the judge that I couldn't dress myself. Meanwhile, my attorney instructed me to wear proper attire. The cab driver was my angel who told my aid he wasn't leaving without me. The driver didn't know about my adamance to wait for me. The cab driver also shared how some people don't even belong in the ward. How did he know I didn't belong there? He revealed that some patients escape at the opened iron gate down the road. The doctors can't go after you for liability issues. I just stayed quiet and listened.

While in the court house, one of the patients told me that he is Jesus. I'm thinking, *that's cool*. I tell him, "Guess what? I'm Jesus in a female version." Again, another metaphor that is not meant to scare you, so kindly keep reading. I meant to say Christ lives in my heart. No one said the Holy Spirit within me was male or female. *So why discriminate?* I thought to myself. I probably scared this guy and he thought I was fanatical, as if he wasn't. Did he forget we were both in a mental facility and considered insane? He decided to move his seat. Even better.

I also contemplated running in the next election and possibly working towards becoming the first female president. Meanwhile, I barely follow politics. Looking back, I remember everything I said, but my imagination was running wild. Perhaps escaping reality was my coping mechanism. Or perhaps I was really bipolar and I had a hard time admitting this. One girl in the hospital told me she was Obama's daughter. That's great, because I'm running to be the first female president. I was in the right place. My brain was definitely hijacked. At least I wasn't passing judgment.

I was still waiting to see the judge. I looked out the window and saw the opened iron gate that was mentioned in passing by the cab driver. I thought to myself, *Is this escape really possible?* I noticed my nurse aide was not in proximity. Perhaps she went to the ladies' room. The guard who was by the front entrance was not standing by the door. I felt like Peter in the Bible, where the guard was not at the prison entrance and the angel guided him to quickly leave! I walked to the iron gate and as soon as I was far enough, I heard the staff calling my name, "Ava, come back!" That is when I started to run faster toward the exit.

I felt like Peter when he was being sent to trial. Acts 12:6-10, "Peter was sleeping between two soldiers, bound with two chains, and sentries stood guard at the entrance. Suddenly an angel of the Lord appeared and a light shone in the cell. He struck Peter on the side and woke him up. 'Quick get up!' He said, and the chains fell off Peter's wrists. Then the angel said to him, 'Put on your clothes and sandals.' And Peter did so. 'Wrap your cloak around you and follow me,' the angel told him. Peter followed him out of the prison, but he had no idea that what the angel was doing was really happening; he thought he was seeing a vision." This is exactly how I felt when Paul and the angel passed the first and the second guards and came to the iron gate leading to the city. It opened for them by itself, and they went through it. When they had walked the length of one street, suddenly the angel left him." I too saw the iron gates and exited. I thought, *Am I dreaming? This was too easy.*

I ran as far as my legs would take me and then I knocked on some stranger's door and asked if I could use her phone. I had to explain that I left the hospital and needed to reach my attorney. She brought me a cordless phone through the screen door as I waited outside. Of course, my attorney wasn't in the office. She was in court all morning. I explained, "I will just wait outside until my lawyer returns my call." Not knowing how long that would take and exhaustion taking over every part of my body, I fell asleep on the lawn. Luckily the weather was beautiful and the grass was nicely manicured. The sunshine felt so warm, like a blanket, and the slight subtle breeze comforted me. When I opened my eyes, I still wasn't dreaming. I asked to call my attorney again. Finally, the secretary was able to reach my attorney. The administrative assistant told me to come to her office and sought a retainer of $7,500.

I didn't have any money on me and I thought to myself, how will I make it to my attorney's office. I walked further to the main road and stumbled upon a bus stop. I hopped on and let the bus driver know I had no money on me but needed to get to the closest Chase bank. This must have been another angelic driver to allow me to ride for free. A few strangers on the bus helped me understand how to transfer buses to reach my main destination which was the 666 building. When I arrived at the Chase bank, I showed them my passport and license. I never surrendered my passport and license when admitted to the mental hospital. We did have one patient in the hospital who was a kleptomaniac, but my belongings remained safe under my pillow.

From the hospital I had called my Chase bank to initiate a high security alert. I needed to make sure Robert would not be able to access my account unless my ID was provided. I had also called the cable company from the hospital and closed my account. I had to make sure Robert wouldn't ruin my credit. I withdrew the $7,500 for my attorney and treaded towards the 666 building. I ate lunch at a Kosher deli, which I learned about from another patient. I was coincidentally in the same town she told me about. Sometimes I think I'm vegan, vegetarian, gluten free and I go on various health kicks. Nothing wrong with changing things up occasionally. I don't want a fanatical food lifestyle either; it's all about a healthy balance with proper boundaries.

I saw a hungry homeless person and I handed him my lunch. When I looked back to see where he went, he vanished. *Perhaps I just entertained an angel* I thought to myself. Hebrews 13:2 says, "Do not forget to show hospitality to strangers, for by so doing some people have entertained angels without knowing it."

Once I arrived at my lawyer's office, I had her call my husband to persuade him to sign the post prenuptial agreement. I still didn't want to end the marriage. She called him and informed him that I'm in her office and wanted to see if he would sign the agreement. He responded with, "She escaped the mental hospital! I got an order of protection against her. She can no longer return or she will be arrested." He also added a deadbolt to the front door and changed the door locks. He must think I'm Houdini, an escape artist, illusionist and stunt performer magician. I thought to myself, *Wow, I just got evicted from my home*. I told my attorney to serve him divorce papers instead, as he left me no choice. My lawyer suggested getting in touch with a therapist that can represent me in court - Dr. Anderson who lives in Great Neck. I told my attorney how I just escaped and tried to cancel my health insurance to be released. The hospital called my parents and told them my insurance was dropped and my mom gave my husband the money to reinstate it. I may be considered insane but I was still clever. Alcatraz was the most secure prison of its time that was considered inescapable, until three daring men made a successful attempt.

I'm reminded of the scripture Matthew 19:26, "but with God all things are possible." It is amazing how, when you put your mind to something, even the impossible becomes possible with the guidance of Christ. Meditate on God's promises to prevail in the darkest storms like an Eagle.

I decided to Uber to Great Neck and stay in a quaint contemporary five-star Andrew Hotel. Since I didn't have a car, I wanted to stay close to the therapist's office. I made an appointment to meet with Dr. Anderson at 1pm the very next day. I checked into the hotel and the front desk attendant asked for my identification. I told him, "I need to check in with an alias name because I don't want my ex-husband to find me." However, the clerk was not allowed to do check me in without identification. After telling him my story he suggested paying in cash to avoid collecting all my personal information. *Beautiful!* I quickly checked into my cozy stylish room. I was relieved to finally have the chance to shave my hairy legs and underarms. The hospital prohibited sharp items to prevent self-harm. Even the drawstrings from my juicy couture sweatpants were removed. After taking a long, relaxing shower, I finally felt like a human again. I called the airlines to check the details of their next flight to Punta Cana, Dominican Republic. I still had my passport and my reservations in place. I couldn't wait. Everything was still going according to the plan. At least I thought so. I went to the New York Sports Club for which I had a free guest pass thanks to my hotel stay. I took two Zumba classes in a row. Music and dance really recharged my soul after what seemed like an eternity of ordeals. I then went to eat at Bareburger where I devoured this delicious bison lettuce wrap. Chase bank and the railroad were walking distance from my hotel as were these quaint eateries.

The next morning, I decided to head over to the bank. I realized I may need more money for my trip. I was using pay phones and selecting *67 before dialing to prevent caller ID from appearing, so I wouldn't be traced. At the Chase bank I was unable to press *67 when I called my younger sister Raquel to see if she could wire me some money because my parents were in Paris at the time. My mom had about $3,000 of my Wig Boutique money since we worked together. Within seconds, I spotted cops entering the bank. I ran out the doors like Speedy Gonzalez. It appeared as if I was being chased because I held up the bank. My newsboy hat flies off my head and I start heading towards the woods. I used to jog at the nature preserves and I loved getting lost in the hiking trails. In fact, my life resembled a maze. I would frequently get lost and always find my way out.

Just as I was about to reach the woods, someone pushed from the back losing my balance. I landed on the floor with this sexy cop on top, handcuffing me. It was kind of fun, I must admit. I like being chased after. In many facets of life, I am hard to get, like being celibate before marriage. I asked the attractive cop if he has a girlfriend. He responded, "Yes." I tell him, "That's okay. Do you want another one?" I desperately needed his help. The female cop called me disgusting. Well of course I was. I'm sure she would pull out similar tactics out of her bag if she was trying to avoid being put back in a mental institution.

The cops searched my hotel room and saw my travel itinerary spread out on my bed. They also found a folder with my passport and loose cash. The cops began to realize that there was merit to my story- I truly was trying to escape from my husband who had me wrongfully admitted into a mental facility and I was trying to go on a vacation to clear my head. The attractive police officer came back and said, "I believe her story." So perhaps a little flirting did help. At first, I thought he was trying to be sneaky and hide something in his pocket like in the movies. Unless we are filming this very moment.

My ex-husband used to sell illegal fireworks during the 4th of July. Our neighbor Nick bought a box of fireworks and was inquiring where the fireworks were being stored. Robert was too clever to be questioned and did not disclose incriminating information. A few days later we had five cop cars arrive at our home to search our garage; thinking Robert had a pallet of explosives for each of them. Robert looked at the officer's name badge and realized he was Nick's older brothers. Not only was Nick our neighbor but also our landscaper who set my ex-husband up. Nick and the officer looked like twins. Luckily for Robert, the other boxes of fireworks were stored elsewhere. The cops left with only one box of explosives. From that day forward we found a new landscaper.

I didn't commit a crime. Yet again, I'm being sent right back to the mental hospital. I almost started hyperventilating because I felt claustrophobic since my hands were handcuffed and the windows remained shut. I imagined once the car door was shut, I was going to suffocate. My mind was playing tricks on me. I kept yelling, "I can't breathe! I can't breathe!" Luckily, I didn't endure a full-blown panic attack because the cop cracked the window open. I mentally pacified my anxiety by telling myself, *calm down, the window is now open.* I almost had a clean getaway. If only I avoided making that call to my younger sister Raquel. Later on, I discovered that the airline red flagged the name Ava Martinez. I wouldn't have gotten past security. I did not commit a crime nor did I pose a danger to anyone else and yet, airlines were instructed to stop me from boarding. The cops were ready to go to any length to catch me.

CHAPTER SEVEN

PATIENT INTAKE FOR DEFENDING MYSELF FROM A POSSIBLE RAPE AND CONVERSATION WITH GOD DIALOG FROM MY CHILDHOOD MOLESTATION.

Balancing life and setting proper boundaries is key to avoid a psychiatric hospital with a straitjacket. I was restrained in a hospital bed because I feared sexual assault. I instructed them to sedate me as I wanted to remain unaware of what would unfold if the staff members raped me. My knuckles were black and blue the next day since I wasn't going to give in without a boxing match. I had warned them not to come near me. I told them, "if you're planning to rape me, I'm letting you know right now. Go right ahead and rape me because my father in heaven is going to take care of you!" I started to verbally cast out all the demons in the room by saying out loud, "I bind and rebuke you Satan in the name of Jesus!" I've been around Christian people long enough to remember they would pray away demons. I never imagined one day I would be praying like this. To be honest, I really didn't know what I was saying. After some research, I discovered that only God has the authority to rebuke the devil. It's important not to repeat what people tell us but to verify it with God's word because many false prophets will try to twist the word and deceive us with it as stated in Matthew 24:11.

We are just called to humble ourselves before God. Resist the devil, and he will flee from us, as stated in, James 4:7. It is the Lord who rebukes Satan, as narrated in Zechariah 3:2 not us.

Even Michael, one of the most powerful of the angels, did not dare to accuse Satan, but rather said, "The Lord rebuke you" (Jude 1:9). God has given us his full armor to stand against evil (see Ephesians 6:10-18). The most effective weapons we have against the devil is our faith, wisdom, and knowledge of God's word. I also researched and learned in Matthew 16:19, "whatever you bind on earth will be bound in heaven, and whatever you loose on earth will be loosed in heaven." The expressions "bind" and "loose" were common to Jewish legal phraseology meaning to declare something forbidden or to declare it allowed. So, I binded and rebuked Satan, not truly understanding what I was saying.

Once my hands were behind my back, I surrendered. Slowly the medication flowed through my veins, rendering me drowsy. When I woke up, I asked the nurse, "Did anyone rape me." She told me I was disgusting probably because I gave them permission to rape me, not without a fight. She proceeded to tell me I wasn't raped. I never gave them permission because I said, "go right ahead" meaning, "you're not intimidating me and I'm not scared." I made them aware of the consequences if they tried. I saw a perverted guy passing my room who probably felt he missed out. Yuck.

The next day, I was transferred from a co-ed facility to a women's only facility. I was told the doctors wanted to do an intake, which entails gathering medical information from patients. The only other time I heard this word *intake* was from a friend at church. Elizabeth recommended that I join a Wildflower retreat for women who have been sexually abused. Elizabeth said that, at the retreat, they would do an *intake* and I would relive my childhood experience by retelling the story. I'm transparent, and I was not ashamed of sharing my experience with sexual abuse. I told myself many years ago that there is a high statistic of sexual abuse in this world and I happen to fall into that category. My experience only made me a stronger person. As a victim of sexual abuse, I learned to be self-reliant.

Later in life, I discovered the devil was also self-reliant. It was imperative that I learn how to trust God more than myself. That wasn't an easy shift to surrender. All the hurdles that I encountered in my life made me a fierce woman who is capable of fending for herself. If I didn't tend to my needs, no one else would. Relinquishing control proved to be challenging. I called Elizabeth from the hospital and asked her if she was referencing this particular moment in life, that the intake would take place in the hospital. Almost as if she had a premonition that this was going to happen to me and God was preparing me. Elizabeth was perplexed and couldn't comprehend anything I had said. In fact, she seemed slightly petrified with silence on the other side of the phone. She hung up the phone on me. Perhaps because I was calling from a mental hospital and my story sounded bizarre. If someone called me up out of the blue and asked me a question like the one I had thrown at her, I would have blocked their name and number.

The doctors gathered in the conference room and began the *intake* with a myriad of questions. Why did you attack the doctors? Why did you give them permission to molest you? I finally found the perfect opportunity to explain myself and all the slightly eccentric comments I may have made. So I shared that when I first arrived, one of the patients had asked me, "Why are you wearing your diamond tennis bracelet?" She explained, "When they checked you into the hospital, they were supposed to take all of your personal belongings." The only personal belongings I retained were my license and my passport. I tucked my ID under my pillow. I knew these were crucial to execute my plan of making it to Punta Cana, Dominican Republic and escape from the chaos that the world seemed to be piling up on me. I further revealed that the patient told me that the staff would rape me and take my bracelet. She told me she conceived while in the hospital by an unwarranted staff member and they took her baby from her. She shared that she was a queen in her country. I thought to myself, *my father is a king.* So maybe she was talking in metaphors. Was she really telling me the truth or was she partially hallucinating?

Considering the fact that I met her in a psychiatric ward, maybe I should have taken her words with a pinch of salt. In this world nothing surprises me anymore. I've seen enough movies to know anything is possible. Who would believe me if I was raped? I'm certified crazy now. She also told me I would encounter a girl that would be a cherry on top of the disgusting cake that was my life at that point. She told me I would know exactly who she is when I saw her. I walked into my new sleeping quarters, which was a fancy name for a mattress on the floor. When I began to dust my space, my roommate came out from under her sheets because I was disturbing her sleep. Immediately I thought, this is the girl the other patient must have been talking about. My roommate had long black hair with bangs and dark tan skin. She looked like a clone of my Mexican friend Carolina, the social worker whose husband had me admitted. My roommate loudly got out of her bed and was ready to attack me. That is when the doctors stormed into my room and I was convinced that I was going to be raped because the patient was right about everything that would happen, chronologically.

I explained to the doctors in the room, "When I was a little girl I didn't know how to say, 'No' to my abuser who molested me. I felt so empowered and fearless when I told the staff, If you do touch me be prepared for the consequences." So, Elizabeth was right. I relived my childhood and retold my story at an intake. I felt fearlessly stronger than before. I experienced a sense of freedom as I was unshackled from my past after this experience.

Before the hospital incident, during one of my private sessions without my husband, the therapist asked me about my childhood. He said we were going to talk with God and to respond candidly.

Q. God, where were you when Ava was molested?

A.   He was in my heart.

Q. God, why didn't you protect her from this? She was only a child.

A.   He did! God made sure I didn't tell my parents because God knew my parents were not going to believe me and the disappointment would have rubbed salt on the wound.

Q. God, couldn't Ava have found someone else to share her secret with?

A. I did. I shared it with another girl who was my age at the time. She was my godfather's niece, related to his wife's side of the family and she confided that he touched her inappropriately also.

Q. God, where were her parents when this occurred for no one to even know?

A. My parents were having a BBQ outside and he would pretend he left his glasses upstairs and he would ask me to get it for him when no one was in the house.

Q. God, why couldn't Ava eventually find someone to confide in?

A. I eventually told my parents when I turned 16. He came to my house and tried to kiss me in the hallway as he was walking toward the restroom. I pushed him away because I was bigger and older.

Q. God, why did you wait so long to allow Ava to find her voice?

A. I told my parents the next day because I was able to handle myself. My father acted in disbelief just as I had suspected. I was glad I didn't tell him when I was younger.

Q. God, how else have you protected Ava?

A. God let me know, my godfather is being punished for what he did to me. My sister Janice called me one day and shared he is in jail for charges of molestation in Florida.

Q. God, what do you want to tell Ava now?

A. I'm the special one because he chose me to bring my family to Christ.

I was blown away by our session. An interactive dialog session with God himself. That was the best $125 I had ever spent. The responses just rolled off the top of my tongue as if the words weren't coming from within me but from my superior deity. Even I was surprised with the super natural responses I spoke.

At that point, the therapist said I was self-reliant because of my childhood experience. He told me the devil was self-reliant. I never would have made that connection from my past without this therapist. I never thought I was affected by my childhood. I just thought I was part of an ugly statistic because I always knew we lived in a fallen world. I thought my childhood abuse just made me independently stronger by being able to fend for myself against strangers. The therapist had me take a pencil and break it in half as a visual promise to myself to never be self-reliant again. He shared the devil was self-reliant and was casted out of heaven. I had to remind myself, God will fight my battles as promised in Exodus 14:14.

When I left his office, I felt so liberated. That same day, I almost ran over a family walking behind my car when pulling out of a parking lot. Luckily, that wasn't how my day ended. I must have pissed off Satan, to try to startle me. I also learned in therapy that I had married someone like my mother. My mother was a loving, controlling disciplinarian. My dad, however, was a people-pleaser and a push-over. I was attracted to the way I was raised by my mother because we had order, structure and stability, and I felt safe with that. One day, someone told me I should have married someone like my dad. My parents do have a nice marriage. Nice girls usually like bad boys and bad boys usually like nice girls that they can control. Opposites attract. But now I'm ready to meet someone who is unlike either of my parents. I need someone with a balanced temperament.

The doctors moved me to the women's only facility after our intake. I had a nurse follow me around for the next two days to make sure I wouldn't harm anyone else because I got physical with the doctors. Both co-ed and women's only facilities seemed like unsafe spaces to me. I saw a fight unfold in the women's facility and strands of hair flew around like confetti. I was shocked to see the security didn't break up their fight. The male security waited till the brawl subsided to restrain the two girls. The fight continued for a good 5 minutes. I thought I was watching a live UFC match. I was just waiting for one of the girls to tap out due to a submission. I made a mental note of this event so I could be prepared if I was ever thrown in the same situation. I was waiting for the referee to stop the fight if the girl got knocked out or was no longer intelligently defending herself. My husband had bought me boxing gloves and trained me a few times, which explains my black and blue knuckles. I wasn't wearing my boxing gloves.

This Jamaican girl liked my $50 Havana flip flops I was wearing, so I gave them to her. I noticed that she began to get aggressive at times. I told her, "Don't mistake my kindness for weakness because I beat up a few staff members in the co-ed facility and that's how I ended up in this women's facility." She thought about it twice and quickly turned 180 degrees. Once she knew she couldn't intimidate me, she didn't want the challenge.

People who act strong are actually pretty weak. That's why they bully people who they think are weaker than them. This didn't stop her from trying again another day.

One day she smelt an offensive fart odor and assumed I did it. I've seen my sister-in law get outraged on a bus that was transporting us to the Hershey Resort from the Hersheypark. My sister-in-law forgot she used to change diapers and her three Chihuahuas poop indoors on wee wee pads. But that isn't offensive. I never understood why people would become so outraged with certain orders. As if they never farted before. The Jamaican girl was ready to attack me. I quickly told her, "I didn't fart. It came from the ceiling." She started laughing. I was dead serious! Once, I was in the same spot she was standing in and that offensive fart smell arrived. I thought to myself, *where did that come from?* I was the only one standing there. I looked up. I'm convinced that the smell sprays out from the ceiling to see how different people react. More mental research data for them to gather. Regardless of the merit of my conclusions, I knew that my thoughts prevented her from attacking me.

The Jamaican girl made her third attempt the day before my release. From her body language, I knew she wanted to dump her anger on someone. I looked at her and told her, "Don't even think about it!" As if I could read her mind, "I'm being released tomorrow and if you attack me, I can't fight you back because they will detain me longer." She smiled at me, took her drink and splashed it on the girl next to me. The Lord gave me a spiritual gift, discernment of thoughts. The Jamaican girl struck out three times and yet, I made it to home base untouched. I didn't know how good I was at baseball. Refer to scripture verse 1 Corinthians 12:7-11 to find out what your spiritual gift is.

One evening I was watching TV and one of the patients decided to just shut it off. She wanted to sleep in the den area. I got up and turned the television back on. I'm not sure where she was going with this stunt she pulled, as the TV curfew hadn't begun yet. Her room doors were obviously open to her if she was seeking some silence. Before I could even turn my back, I was shoved to the ground. I thought to myself quickly, *if I fight this chick, the doctors will not stop it.* Immediately, the nurses jumped behind the counter to protect themselves. They didn't know what was going to happen next and neither did I. I decided to just stay on the ground. It takes two people to fight and I wasn't going to give her the satisfaction. When the Doctors came the next day to evaluate me and find out what happened they were so impressed. I was able to hold back from attacking back in self defense. They told me I was making great progress. I couldn't believe it myself. The absence of a reaction diffuses everything. I'm a true advocate now, it takes two to fight. Let them fight by themselves. When you gain control over your emotions and feelings, you wield true power. Controlled and regulated responses can be truly intimidating. I'm grateful for the lessons I learned in the mental facility.

A few years ago, I wouldn't have thought twice before attacking back, but I had too much at stake. If a stranger crossed the line with me, I was always ready to strike back. This response stemmed from being molested and I felt like I had to make sure that no one else took advantage of me. Much easier to handle strangers than people you see on a regular basis. In middle school, a Hispanic girl named Evelyn picked a fight with me because we were both attractive and her friends provoked her. She came toward me unexpectedly and said, "Why are you biting (slang for copying) my style?" Immediately, she shoved me against the locker to prove her strength. I certainly did not back away. We ended up in the principal's office.

Another time in high school, Kenya threw my books on the ground. She attacked me out of nowhere. She was known for being fierce. She cut a student's ponytail in art class for no apparent reason. She threw a random guy off the stair banister and he ended up with a broken arm. By throwing my books, Kenya met her match. I get it, hurting people hurt people. But she didn't know the quiet girl Ava was masking a pain that would take you down like a lion. That's why I never resented what happened to me as a child. I accepted it as my strength that I fostered to protect myself.

Unfortunately, with friends and family I was a people pleaser and taken advantage of because I deeply desired acceptance and approval. Where did that stem from? My older sister Silvia told me I had a big nose when I was younger. I used to squish my nose against the wall thinking I could make it smaller. I told my younger son Jonathan the story about my nose because his older brother Louis was making fun of Jonathan's bubble butt. I caught Jonathan rubbing his butt back and forth on the floor. I knew exactly what he was doing. I asked him, "Are you trying to make your butt flatter?" I explained, "Your brother Louis is jealous because I complimented your perky butt." I told Jonathan, "I used to squish my nose against the wall also to make it smaller because my sister said my nose was big." Jonathan replied, "Why mom? Did you have a different nose?" I wanted to laugh. I said, "No honey, I had the same nose." Jonathan understood the depth behind my words and was comforted by my relatable story.

Silvia's favorite words to me were, "You're so stupid." She was constantly correcting my speech, vocabulary and pronunciations. Reading comprehension wasn't my strongest suit either. Perhaps I believed I was not smart, which caused me to doubt myself. She also corrected my manners as if I should automatically know better. I'll give you an example. Once, we were at a small backyard BBQ gathering, near the water and there were grapes on the table. I started picking at the grapes from the stem. She told me, "Must I teach you etiquette? You must take the grapes and put them on a separate plate." Watching too many soap operas led her to live in her own reality show in her head. While that was undoubtedly proper etiquette, she spoke down to me as if we didn't come from the same family. She desired to be extravagant with her rabbit fur coats in high school as if they were mink and wore cocktail rings as if she lived on an estate. When have you seen anyone in your high school wearing fur coats and cocktail rings to class? Exactly, me neither. Let's just say my sister was extraordinary. She currently lives in a $7million home.

The hospital was required to provide me with The Patients' Bill of Rights upon my arrival. However, I had to request them. The patients equipped me with the skills I needed to inculcate to survive. They shared what attorney to hire, when not to sign release papers and so on. The nurses tried to intimidate me, as if

I were ignorant. Knowledge is power, so I couldn't be manipulated with my newfound peers. One of the nurses coerced me to take the medication, so I tucked it under my tongue. She wanted to look in my mouth with a flashlight. Was she kidding me? I ignored her and went to my bathroom and split it out. I have the right to refuse treatment used for mental research unless ordained by a judge. One way or another I had to get out of there.

A patient from the hospital advised me not to sign the release papers so they're held liable if anything happens to me. The nurses lied to me that I couldn't leave unless I signed. I made a quick phone call to my attorney and he told me, "Your signature is not a requirement to leave." The nurses definitely tried to intimidate me by delaying my release so I would sign the release papers. Finally, on one evening, the staff told me that if I did not leave the property by a certain time, I would be readmitted. I couldn't believe what she just told me. I was almost scared to get in the taxi cab because I was afraid it would be another trick. Would he drive me to another mental health facility and fabricate another story? It wasn't the yellow cab I was accustomed to either. I was skeptical but I had no choice. I got inside and asked to get dropped off at the Grand Lux Cafe restaurant at the Roosevelt Field Mall to mislead anyone who might have been following me.

I couldn't risk people knowing where I was staying. I walked into the bathroom and changed my clothing so no one would recognize me when I left the restaurant. I entered the mall and treated myself at a blow-out bar to get my hair straightened. Then I went to Victoria's Secret and purchased some new underwear for my trip to the Dominican Republic, Punta Cana, Paradisus. I inquired about getting a mobile phone without a name associated with the number to avoid being traced. The salesperson at Metro PCS said, "As long as you pay cash at one of our locations each month, we wouldn't need your personal information." I couldn't risk the chance of getting caught again. I was released, but it feels like I was still being followed.

CHAPTER EIGHT

LOVE NOTES LEFT FROM THE ELF OF THE SHELVE AND HIS REINDEER PET.

I went to Toys R Us in Carle Place, to purchase a bike so I could ride it to my parents' house in Massapequa. My mom and dad were in Paris and while I was in possession of their house keys. I could stay there in the meantime. Strangely enough, the salesperson didn't want to sell me the floor model bike. I told the salesperson, "If you don't sell me the floor model bike, I'm going to make a big scene in this store." He didn't think I was serious. I started yelling out loud, "This is discrimination because I want to purchase this bike and I have the money for it." I then started yelling, "Hello, is there anyone here? Who can sell me this bike?" Finally, another salesperson came and I was finally enjoying proper service. The cops entered the ToysR Us but I knew they couldn't arrest me, as I broke no law. The bike was a pink cruiser with a rear storage rack to place my belongings. I bought my son the Pet Reindeer from The Elf on the Shelf since Christmas was around the corner.

I didn't raise my children to believe in Santa Claus. I raised my boys to celebrate Jesus' birthday on Christmas Day. I would have a birthday ice cream cake spelled in gel icing, "Happy Birthday Jesus." If the Jewish people didn't teach their kids about Santa, why should I? I would rather teach my kids about the Passover and the menorah, which are facts with historical relevance. My heritage of Puerto Rican culture was to celebrate the three kings that traveled with gifts to give to baby Jesus. Our society has regressed to a state where we are teaching our kids to lie through fairy tales; upon finding out the truth they are devastated over being lied to for years. Nobody likes being cheated. Then we do it again with the tooth fairy. I'm guilty of having Ratoncito Perez, similar to the Tooth Fairy, delivering money under my boys' pillows in exchange for their tooth. The folktale of Ratonicto Perez originated in Madrid in 1894 and became a part of the Hispanic American Culture.

Almost everyone in the elementary school was discussing about this elf. My son came to me and wanted to know when the elf would come to our home. If I didn't bring Santa Clause into my home, why would I compromise my faith to now have an elf? I decided to turn the elf into God's messenger and I would hide biblical love notes around the house. I didn't want to conform to the world because in John 15:19 states, "As it is, you do not belong to the world, but I have chosen you out of the world." I don't need others to understand my traditions, just God. I truly enjoyed being different and creative to incorporate the truth to the best of my ability. I hope to be a balanced person and not a fanatical extremist. Others may differ in perspective.

The lady in front of me at ToysR Us was purchasing a few gifts for her children for Christmas. She was going to put them on layaway. I felt so bad. I offered to pay for it. I gave the salesperson my credit card. The lady was shocked. I told her not to worry, my ex-husband will take care of it. I was using his Disney credit card. I then left the Toys R' US department store on my new bike with my magical reindeer elf pet. I had a 14-mile ride ahead of me. I stopped at the nearest eatery to warm myself. I ordered some food and when I was done eating, I went to pay for my meal. To my surprise my credit card was declined. How embarrassing! I left the food joint with a verbal promise of paying it back another day. Never in my life did I leave a place without paying.

I continued my journey toward my parents' home in Massapequa. I was riding with no hands and still managed to balance the bike perfectly. If only I could balance my life just as good. I felt like cars were following me from different corners and avenues. I know that sounds delusional. I can only conclude, I never signed the release papers and they were keeping an eye on me. The hospital would be held liable if anything were to happen to me. I hear cars beeping at me as I continue to ride with no hands. I was racing with my body tucked low to accelerate. I heard more cars honking down each block I passed. I didn't realize how entertaining I was. I started riding standing up, as my glutes began to hurt. I felt as if I took a vigorous cycle class. But boy, my hands were getting cold. I finally made it to Massapequa safely.

I began writing a letter from the rein deer elf to deliver a note that read, "You found my letter. Congratulations! This Christmas remember Deuteronomy 4:29, "Seek the Lord your God, you will find him if you look for him with all your heart and all your soul." I never stopped trying to find you when you moved away. Just remember during Christmas that it is better to give than receive. Although, I'm sure you will enjoy all the gifts God provides for you each year. Philippians 4:17 says, when we give to others, we benefit because God appreciates and sees what we have done. Remember to always be a cheerful giver."

Every time the elf flew to a different location, he would leave another note which said, "Love conquers all." In 1 Corinthians 13:4, "Love is **patient**, love is **kind**. It does not **envy**, it does not **boast**, it is not **proud**. It is not **rude**, it is not **self-seeking**. It is not **easily angered**, it keeps no record of wrongs. Love does not delight in evil but rejoices with the truth. It always protects, always trusts, always hopes, always perseveres." Which of these underlined bold words fits your personality? Which of these words may you need more work on? Just remember Jesus Loves you and knows your heart better than anyone else. Rest in his peace tonight, as we look forward to Christmas. Let's count down the days.

I had taken Jonathan and Louis to see the nutcracker on my visitation day. I incorporated this note from the elf that read, "Did you know the nutcracker is a classical ballet? I hope you enjoyed watching the play as much as I did at Hofstra University. The traditional nutcracker can be found all over Germany. I especially enjoyed the music. What did you think of the evil mouse? Did the nutcracker do a good job in protecting the girl? The Lord is faithful and he will strengthen and protect you from the evil one, just like the nutcracker. It's God's promise in 2 Thessalonians. Have a Happy New Year and enjoy all the gifts Christ delivers to you both."

Sometimes my children's visitations were at the public library and I had the elf leave a love note in their backpack that read, "I want to share how proud I am of both of you at school. It is not the grades that determine who you will be, but the effort that you put in counts more. Grades don't define you but your relationship with Christ does. Here is a Test Quiz question. 1 Corinthians 13:13, "But these three things remain: Faith, hope and love. But the greatest of these is _____?" Faith, Hope or Love? Fill in the blank. Check your Bible to find the right answer. Jesus loves when you spend time in his word. Don't forget to pray before bedtime. Make sure your homework is done and never stop learning. Have a goodnight."

My parents took an earlier flight to NY from Paris when they learned about my hospital admission. They had plans of going directly to Florida to celebrate Thanksgiving with my other sisters, but they wanted to make sure I was okay in New York. When my parents arrived, I noticed my mother seemed indifferent toward me. I asked her, "Let's go for a manicure and pedicure like we normally do." She told me, "No." I said, "Why not?" I also asked her, "Where is my Wig Boutique money?" She wasn't ready to give it to me. Which was also very unusual. In the 15 years we worked together she never took a dime from me. But at that moment, she refused to give me my money.

I felt like a hostage in my mothers house. She was fearful I would escape again. I went outside to ride my bike and allow fresh air to rejuvenate me. However, she started banging on the glass window to attract my attention and asked me to come back inside. Was she kidding me? I suddenly needed permission to ride my own bike. I felt stuck in my worst nightmare, because the mother I knew wouldn't act like this.

CHAPTER NINE

ATTEMPTED KIDNAPPING FROM THE MOVIE THEATER.

The next day, I knew I either had to get out of my mother's house or relinquish control over my own life. I told her I was going to the movie theater which was within walking distance. Both Regal UA and Showcase Cinema were close by. I walked into the Showcase Cinema and I sat by myself. The theater was practically empty. Shortly after, the theater got packed. I was uncertain whether I was still being followed. I didn't entertain those thoughts and shunned them as paranoia. The movie was entertaining.

After the movie, I walked out and found myself in the midst of a crowd. I walked into the ladies' room where I heard them talking about how the cops were there for a kidnapping. I think nothing of it and continue to wash my hands. As I walk out of the restroom, the cops approach me. The officer asks me a few questions, "What is your name? What movie were you watching?" I was hesitant to respond. I kept asking, "What is going on?" but they wouldn't tell me. My oldest sister and my mother were at the theater too. This was getting quite weird. I didn't know what was happening here. *Why are my mother and sister at the theater?* I ask myself. I answered the officer's few simple questions and he instructed my sister and my mother to drive me home. "No detours" the cop told them. I couldn't make sense of this; I was able to put the pieces together eventually. My sister and my mother were plotting to abduct me and admit me to Stony Brook Psychiatric Hospital against my will.

I remembered some patients' stories about how their parents controlled them by shifting them from hospital to hospital. My oldest sister was always jealous of the relationship I had with my mother. I was born on Silvia's exact birthday. We were seven years apart. What a lucky number. I took away her spotlight from her birthday celebrations because we had to share that day. We were complete opposites. She loved cake and I loved ice cream. My sister couldn't wait to get me out of the family picture. My mom and Silvia became best buddies, bonding at my expense. The Lord protected me because the cops made sure I was taken back to my mother's house and not another hospital. I remember the patients instructing me not to sign the discharge papers because the hospital would be held liable if anything were to happen to me. Perhaps the phone lines were tapped. Only that could explain how the cops found me. I felt the Lord's protection shielding me as their scheme did not work. Isaiah 54:17 reads, "No weapon forged against you will prevail." So thankful for the Lord's promises.

The next day, my mother told me that I needed to go to St. Joseph Hospital in Bethpage. I told my mom, "I'm fine. I don't need to go to any hospital." But if she persists, I decided to comply after my 40th birthday because I had an event planned. I had called a few friends and patients from the hospital who were released and we had plans to meet at the Swing 46 in NYC. I wanted to celebrate my birthday and my divorce at this Jazz venue, Supper Club. I told my parents they could come if they wanted to. I didn't understand the urgency to re-admit me again. At least let me celebrate my birthday with jazz music and swing dance lessons.

My mom ignored my request and insisted that I must go back to the hospital. She immediately took me to the emergency room. She started crying at the check in window like some actress. Those tears were surprising, considering it was a fabricated story. She should have gotten a Grammy award for this performance. She told the nurses, "My daughter is not well and you need to evaluate her." While I kept clarifying that "I'm perfectly fine." I explained to them, "I was released and I don't see why she wants me readmitted." Regardless, they decided to have me under observation. I was waiting to see the doctors so they can confirm that I'm completely fine. My mother belonged in the hospital more than me for her crazy imagination. It's fascinating how some people do more harm when they assume they are helping you.

I told the nurse, "I'm going to the vending machine to get a candy bar." As I walk down the hallway, I get on the elevator and I find the exit sign. I quickly hopped onto a bus and disappeared. I was not going to allow them to readmit me. I had big plans for my 40th birthday. That was another clever escape if I say so myself. I felt like James Bond. He is so sexy. When I returned to my mother's house, I spotted an ambulance and a cop car. They approached me, asking me a myriad of questions. I didn't hear a word they were saying because I kept thinking, *I better run. How can I make this escape?* While I was contemplating what to do next, they grab my arms and force me into the ambulance. *Oh great, here we go again.*

I tried flirting with the ambulance driver so he does not take me back to the hospital. I made him laugh a few times. My life was one big joke, and I wanted to crack up too. Laughing was my defense mechanism to mask any weakness or vulnerability. I remember one time, my ex-husband was upset over something and I just laughed because I didn't want to cry. This made Robert even more angry. That wasn't my intention at all.

The ambulance took me back to the mental facility. Everyone was surprised and elated at the same time at my return. As I arrived, I sarcastically said, "Hey guys, it's me again. I missed you; I couldn't stay away." I use to lead the the Zumba classes in the mornings. During music therapy with working out from our chairs, I would do the advanced version of the same workout. I enjoyed the adult coloring sessions too. Occasionally, the patients fought over the colored pencils. The social workers used to organize games for us to play. I learned the card game *Apples to Apples*. We also had a relaxation room with soothing lotions from *Bath and Body Works*. A Rubik's Cube and a Pilates ball made the relaxation room a fun place to be at. I could get one whole color uniformly on the Rubik's Cube. Surprisingly, I retained my skills. I promised my son Louis a Rubik's Cube as a gift.

By the time I was released from the hospital, my son Louis figured out how to get every color coordinated on the Rubik's Cube within one minute. I was so impressed by his need to wow me. A month later, my pastor at Centerpoint conducted a sermon while arranging all the colors on the Rubik's Cube. I still get so dumbfounded when the Lord adds up all these little details in my life with something as insignificant as a Rubik's Cube. The sermon had more meaning because of my recent personal experiences.

I contracted a slight yeast infection. I requested the nurses to get me a consultation with a gynecologist. I didn't realize they didn't have over the counter medication available unless brought in by a family member. The gynecologist visits the hospital only once a week. When I finally met the Doctor, I explained to him that I had an IUD Miranda inserted and I believed that was causing my infections and I wanted it removed. The doctor feels me inside while the female nurse stands next to him. He didn't bring the instrument needed to remove it. I kept thinking, *what type of a traveling doctor doesn't come prepared?* I had to reschedule another visit with this doctor which I was dreading because he didn't seem credible.

The following week, the doctor visited me again. This time he didn't have the instrument with him yet again, but he insisted on removing my IUD with his fingers. I kept telling myself, *unbelievable, he comes twice without the instrument. This pervert is touching me and thinks that I'm a mental patient and he can take advantage of me. Who would believe me? I'm considered insane.* Tears rolled off my face as his fingers slipped inside me. He acted annoyed because he realized I wasn't enjoying the experience. The female nurse seemed unaware that it is nearly impossible to remove a t-shaped piece of plastic inserted in my uterus. What's the point of having a female assistant in the room during my pelvic examination when she acted invisible. Perhaps she didn't want to lose her job, just doesn't care, or is ignorant. Everyone has to feed their family I suppose, doesn't mean it has to be at someone else's expense. Well, I hope he enjoyed his cheap thrill.

In the Middle Ages, it was often the norm for a woman to be examined by midwives, nurses or other females. By the early 1800s, pelvic exams began to be performed by male physicians. During this period, chaperones were used because of the allegations that emerged. I never had an issue with a male gynecologist until that day.

Okay now. That was heavy. Let's move onto planning my 40th birthday party. I needed twelve disciples like the Last Supper. Hey, you only turn 40 once in a lifetime. The patients and I began sketching the dresses we would wear for the event. This kept us sanely entertained. I just had to make sure I wouldn't have someone betray me at the party bus like Judas did at the Last Supper. I would write down the names of who I would consider mingling with. Occasionally, I would go back to my notebook, cross their names out and replace it with someone else. Especially if they were acting insane.

CHAPTER TEN

RELEASED FROM THE MENTAL HOSPITAL ON GOOD MERIT. ANOTHER CAR ACCIDENT. TIME TO UPGRADE MY LIFE.

After doing my time, I refused to go back to my parents' house. The doctors kept enquiring where I would stay if I get released. The therapist stated that they couldn't release me unless they knew where I would be staying. Did I sign over my guardianship to the doctors? I wasn't certain about my living situation. But I had no choice but to disclose some sort of location. I called my high school friend Virginia and asked if I could stay with her but she didn't give me a direct answer. I told the doctors I would be staying in a hotel. Our lunch lady could speak Spanish and she told me to call The Safe Center shelter if I wanted a place to stay at. Soon to be homeless and not sure where I would sleep at night, I journaled to keep myself entertained in the meantime.

Monday, 12/21/15 - 7:30am. I just spoke to Dr. Goldmann this morning. I asked him if he would release me so I don't have to see the judge tomorrow. He was honest and as usual, he told me he would keep me longer. He must really like me. I enquired on what basis would he keep me. He replied that he would need to know my housing locality. Now why would I have to tell him where I was going? I told him, "I'm a Gypsy. I traveled abroad, I worked and studied abroad in London, Venice, Amsterdam, Paris, Spain, Egypt and India." I told him if I didn't get married, I would probably be building a hut in Costa Rica and doing missionary work with my church. He reminded me that I have been married for the past 10 years. He didn't like my Gypsy story. I told him he was right. Isn't it cool how I could adapt to whatever circumstance I'm in? He then said, okay let's conclude this session. Meanwhile, I was just getting started. What did he expect me to tell him? My husband changed the door locks to our home and my parents are brainwashed by my ex-husband and my diagnoses.

I had spoken to my accountant and asked if my mom had called him. He said my dad called him. I asked if he would call my dad back to deposit my $3500 for the sales tax. $1500 would remain in my account as an emergency fund just in case I were to be homeless. I mean, a gypsy. He asked if I wanted him to do the sales tax for me. I said, "Yes as long as the funds are available in my account." I normally do my own sales tax to avoid the $275 fee. My accountant tries to be morally correct to the best of his ability. There are no legal loopholes with him.

I also had to call Raquel. She informed me yesterday that she would get in touch with Robert and let him know that I wrote him a letter. I wanted to know if he would allow me to talk to my boys every day. Raquel tried calling him but he didn't pick up. She informed me Robert went to see *Star Wars* at the movie theater with the boys. He informed her that I am only allowed to speak to my boys two times a week. That's crazy. Raquel said that the hospital had ordained that. The hospital is not allowed to disclose my medical information unless I authorize them to. Then we got disconnected. The calls are limited for ten minute intervals. I called my lawyer and left her a message asking if I am only allowed to communicate with my boys twice a week. Not sure who is lying. I was unaware of any imposition of communication restrictions. I was pissed off. I wanted to speak to Dr. Goldmann to see if what my sister said was valid.

"Let's laugh," Glendy told me at breakfast. She told me, "I like the pubic hair on your chin." I thought to myself, *she is nuts.* Instead of crying I just laughed. I told her, "Wait till you see my legs. You could probably braid my hair there too. Soon I will have a unibrow." I just gave Glendy a huge hug for no reason. Then I walked to my bedroom no. 2117 and she followed me. She said, "Let's make some body heat." She's constantly crushing on me. I thought to myself, *I love body heat.* My two boys were my body heat because my husband was always cold to me. You couldn't get warmth from him even if you tried.

At 11am, I met Brian Wellington, my mental healthcare attorney. He informed me that pushing the meds is on the calendar to see the judge but not the discharge request. He was not sure how that happened. So he had to adjourn for another week. This sucks, another week at this place. Next court date was 12/29/15. Brian Wellington clarified that there is no guarantee that the judge would release me either. I guess anything is possible. I wasn't going to get my hopes high. Then I opened my Bible to Romans 3:9 and it says, "What shall we conclude then? Do we have any advantage? Not at all! Romans 3:10-11 says, "As it is written: There is no one righteous, not even one. There is no one who understands; there is no one who seeks God." I concluded, *this is true, no one understands me, but I will continue to seek you, Lord.*

I then spoke to Kathy at the Andrew Hotel to inform her that I will most likely pick up my stuff in security after the new year. I also let her know that the front desk attendant Kevin was very helpful when I stayed there. I apologized for providing a fake name as I was in the middle of an ugly divorce or separation- I didn't know what to call it. But I enjoyed my stay at the hotel and would definitely stay there again in the future. It was a relief to share that with her. Especially since they may have pegged me as a basket case getaway patient. I can picture it now, I'm in psych rehab and I introduce myself as, "Hi, I'm Ava Martinez and I'm a mental patient. My challenges are people suck."

2pm. My parents arrived at the hospital to bring me a coat for my release. I rejected their visit. I have Lisa's coat. Lord, I pray Robert will receive my letter and bring me what I need. A razor and tweezers would be lovely. The small things count more to me these days. I would love to be able to blow dry my hair and wear makeup.

3:45pm. Group Time. The nurse informed me that I would be taking 10 mg of ability. I was so upset. I thought I was going to commence with 7 mg. I just took 5 mg yesterday. I almost objected to the 10 mg but she said I could be released sooner if I take 10 mg. Their goal is to get me to 15 mg. They were nuts. I told them to just sedate me. The medication made me drowsy anyhow. I hate being abused. But this time I just had to be abused this time to get my children back. I was willing to do what it takes.

At night, I heard noises from the other rooms. Some of the patients told me they were given wedgies in the middle of the night. One night I decided to guard the hallway. I let the night shift nurses know if they came out of the office and attempted to bother the patients while they were sleeping, I was going to handle them the way I handled the other doctors in the co-ed facility. I just marched up and down the hallway because my adrenaline was way up. It seemed as though they were daring each other to come out and bother the patients. How old are we? They were daring the nurse to come out and call me out on my bluff. They began to threaten her and claimed if she didn't do the dare, they would harass her. These nurses were bullying the weaker nurse to challenge her boundaries. I firmly said, "I will go in there and take care of you if I hear the nurse in pain for not following your dare." The night shift staff apparently needed some way to entertain themselves at the expense of others to stay awake themselves. These nurses were underpaid. No one came out of the office and no one bothered the patients that night. I then passed out and calloused on the floor from sleep deprivation. All I remember was the nurses wrapping the sheets around me in a special way to lift me off the floor and place me on the bed. The day shift staff was much nicer. But they too had their moments. Monica noted that she found it unusual that I was going on vacation by myself. I explained that I was an independent world traveler before all this. I even got angry with God that my traveling ceased with the words "I Do." I hated my life. I hated being married. I was happier single. I drove a Volvo convertible and I always had money. I took dance lessons at Arthur Murray, Fred Astaire and Rhythmology studio. I also enrolled in Tennis lessons and considered taking up golf. I always had tons of energy and drive in me. I was going to be *Sleeping Beauty* for the next few days on this medication.

Natalie got released that day. She was so good to me. She left me her Abercrombie hooded sweatshirt, body gel, body spray and bath and body works products. Marika called me the same day too but by then, I knew she wasn't a friend. I had been there 47 days and she still hasn't come to visit me. The visiting hours were from 7pm-8pm. Around 7:20pm, the doorbell began to ring and two staff members directed the third staff member to let it ring. I asked Ms. Donald, "Why can't she answer the door when it's visiting hours? She replied, "Don't ask questions." *Oh, I get it. That's how you do it around here.* No reasoning to their madness. It was all a big game to them.

Lord, I wish I had someone to bring me Starbucks. I was so desperate for a nice warm flat white latte. I knew Marika wasn't going to bring me one. I already told her how I like my coffee and that didn't happen. I called an ex-boyfriend from my college years, Aziz. His phone number was etched in my memory. Before cell phones, you either had an address book of contacts or you had to actually memorize phone numbers. I just wanted him to drop off my coffee. I don't really want to see anyone, including my parents. I wouldn't have been surprised if Aziz too disappointed me.

Tuesday 12/22/15 - This morning Lisa surprised me with the coat that she retrieved from my parents from the previous day. Lisa asked me if I wanted to see my parents, as she was in charge of the front desk. She said they brought a jacket for me. I thought it over and decided that I did not want to see them. Lisa was smart enough to get what I needed without coercing me to talk to them. I absolutely love her. She is the best. I finally had something cute for my trip to L.A. Lisa could have her cougar coat back which she had lent me. I can't be a cougar anyhow because I have children. I recently learned this lingo from a millennial. I was considering going to L.A. to visit an old friend.

I decided to call T-Mobile later to facilitate a remote call forward from my business number to my mother's cellular phone to retain my customers. Transferring the Wig Boutique phone number was unnecessarily complex. Two business days were required to make the transfer active.

Lisa had informed me that my mom inquired about my court date that was scheduled for that same day. I was glad they were confused. I informed Raquel that it got adjourned, although she didn't seem to believe me. Even better. I fervently prayed that Dr. Goldmann would release me before the court date so I could see my children for Christmas. At the time of release, I had to procure my medical records to retrieve my personal information, Dr. Goldmann reported.

Dr. Goldmann later informed me that Robert called to schedule a family appointment and something about the accountant. I was certain my accountant would not do anything unethical and I was glad the sales tax got delayed. This way my husband can't steal the income tax money. I told Dr. Goldmann it would be better if Robert and I spoke in person. I did not mind the visit.

I left my accountant a voicemail explaining that my hands were tied. My parents did not deposit any cash into my bank account and as a result, I couldn't go forward with the sales tax. I couldn't decipher why he was speaking to my husband instead of me. Another jerk in my life. Dr. Goldmann also informed me that I could only meet my boys for 15 minutes on Christmas Day at one o'clock. On that day, at 3:30 pm, Hope returned to Zucker Hillside. Her mother tricked her. As soon as she got out of her car, she was rushed involuntarily into the mental hospital by Emergency Medical Technicians (EMTs). She was injected with needles after being forcefully strapped down. She was bruised all over her body. I didn't realize how common this was. When I was finally released, my parents also attempted to put me right back in through an EMT. This scenario seemed to be the norm around here.

I decided to fight for more time with my children. Tina, a staff member suggested requesting to see my boys during a later shift when there are more staff members. If my husband wasn't flexible with the time, I was ready to deny the visit. What's 15 minutes? I was confident God would work this out for me. My husband might have wanted to visit his sister's house later since he always does what's convenient for her schedule. I was unwilling to accommodate that. If evening hours are more conducive for him and will allow me to spend more time with my boys, then that is what I will request.

Jessy wanted to go AWOL. She tried opening the doors by hacking the secured keypads. Around the same time, two big guys were securing the doors. Others were coloring, while I continued to journal. Let's go girls! It's Group Club jamming here. I was stunned to hear the radio station announce that in the

Netherlands you can pay for defensive driving classes with sex. Did I just hear that correctly? Would that include 15- and 16-year-olds? Whatever happened to celibacy until marriage? When did prostitution become legal? I then opened up my Bible to Mark 12:14, "We know that you are a man of integrity. You aren't swayed by others, because you pay no attention to who they are; but you teach the way of God in accordance with the truth. Is it right to pay the imperial tax to Caesar or not?" Lord, thank you for the compliment of integrity. I did try to pay my sales tax on time and was upset when that didn't pan out. I love it when you speak to me.

Wednesday 12/23/15. Dr. Goldmann considered the one o'clock slot to be the best time for a visit from my children. I suggested 3pm when they have the staff shift times. I was hoping that this would allow me to see my boys for half an hour more. I was in despair and inching towards crying. I felt infuriated I was still trapped in the hospital against my will.While sleeping, I dreamt that my parents kept me from walking through the doors of the Family Court. That was scary. Could that end up being my realty one day? Time seemed to crawl like a turtle. I'm usually an optimistic person. Later, Dr. Goldmann discussed with me the possibility of discharging me on Monday or Tuesday since he was on leave on Friday for Christmas. I was excited at the prospect of leaving on Monday. Dear Lord, help me be okay with whatever day it will be. Financially, it was a good thing that I had room and board here. He wanted me to see a psychiatrist upon release.

I had met Brian Wellington, Esq. He informed me that my sister Silvia showed up at court and she could possibly testify against me. I was worried about being abducted and readmitted again. Oh Lord, I am grateful to you that my case was adjourned. I prayed for a Monday release and hoped to see the psychologist on the same day. Otherwise, I would need to find a bus schedule to get back here. I had called my mom to inform her that I had forwarded Wig Boutique number to her cell phone number.

Dear God, It's lonely where I am. No one from the outside visited me except enemies. I left a message for my dad to bring and leave me a Starbucks coffee. Oh, how I've been dreaming about it. Lord, you are my only friend. Can you bring me a cup of coffee?

I've been trying to do laundry since 10am. It was only 3pm. So far, Sara got released. Her real Jewish name is HIYAA. I left a message for Natalie and Robin. I missed them. It's funny how I always remember to call people but no one really remembers to call me. Marika had called me but never visited me. Which hurts. I decided to take a nap as I was hurting. I prefer keeping busy than crying.

Group time - painting. Music - I'm a classic man. My husband was the classic man. I miss him more than my kids because he helped me create them. Now all I have are my children to remember him by. I feel like a widow. As the days got longer, my heart was heavy with weariness. I no longer had the same drive. I forgot I was PMS-ing. Christine told me that she saw a huge difference in me since when I was admitted. She thought I was doing much better. I told her, "No I'm not. I'm an emotional mess

on this medication. I usually dance and am more upbeat."
Genevieve was moving to the groove. I couldn't move. I hate
when people tell me I'm much better now. Yes, mostly every staff
member prefers compliant people, including Christine. I
shouldn't let it bother me. It's that little girl inside me who is
looking for approval still.

Rosemary was talking to herself out loud, angrily. Who am I
to judge? I was talking out loud to myself up and down the
hallways also when I first was admitted. I was venting to me,
myself and I. After dinner, I asked Glendy to pluck out my pubic
hairs on my chin. I laid on my bed as if I were at the spa and she
was able to gently remove my chin hairs. I was so amazed. Then
she gently moved her hands above my little breast. I started
cracking up. I still have a hard time believing she is a lesbian.
Then I put my own hand over my little breast so she doesn't
touch. In exchange for my chin threading, I gave Glendy a
massage by walking on her back. I didn't want to get physical
with her. She may get the wrong vibe.

Nurse Beth then called me over to see if I knew the names of
the staff members I beat up. I told them I didn't know their names.
An internal investigation was underway. She didn't believe they
would give me the names. I just knew that one guy was Asian and
the other was white American and there was one more guy. I
don't know why they didn't investigate before. I was certain they
were just protecting themselves as they know I'm writing my
book.

6:45pm I spoke to my dad. He said he will drop off my coffee,
notebook and nail clippers in the morning. I didn't think the nail

clippers would pass through security. I also asked if he could bring the necklace Jonathan bought me. My dad said it may not be allowed. I decided not to get my expectations high.

Thursday Christmas Eve 12/24/15. 6:20am Robert probably forgot about me. He probably doesn't miss me anymore. People adjust. I had visitors when I first got admitted but then everyone forgot about me. That's how life is. It's a cruel world. I never heard from Monica, Casey or Elma again. I feel like writing off Marika also.

Glendy gifted me a beautiful outfit. Pants, lace tank top and a cardigan sweater. I love it. Thank you, Lord. My dad brought me Starbucks, banana bread, my earrings I wanted for Christmas and the necklace from my son Jonathan, plus a nail file. I was so excited. I'm still my dad's little girl. I then called the 700 club. She prayed for me. Her mighty words were, "If God is for me, who can be against me?"

Today I got to flirt with the new male staff member Jeff. He called me dangerously perceptive. I like that. But the ripped elbow thermals don't work for me. His humor may surpass his fashion skills. Do you know I asked Glendy how come she hasn't given me her parents' phone number? The little stinker finally gave me her digits. Go figure.

Group Time - outside. Global warming. Glendy is scared of what's going on in the world and that the world is out to kill us. The news scares her. She feels responsible for it. Thank you, God, for this beautiful day. I had beautiful thoughts about spending Christmas in NYC and seeing the nutcracker with my children. 10:30pm I'm going to bed with 15 mg of Abilify.

Friday, Merry Christmas 12/25/15. Hospital supplied Dunkin Donuts caffeinated coffee and donuts. I ate a blueberry glaze. Thank God for the coffee they gave me this morning. I went to my room and decided to do yoga in my lace tank top and leggings and then Glendy walked in. She asks, "Why are you so provocative." I began to laugh. *I wish my husband felt that way.* I'll take whatever compliment I can get. Then she asked me to step on her back. Zucker's Foot Spa by Ava.

The staff gave us all gifts. Warm blankets, shower gel, and journals. They even bought two plush dogs for my boys, that I could give to them later. Thank you, Lord. Two stuffed animals with matching blankets and chocolate Santa candy sticks. We listened and hummed to a Christmas caroler playing a guitar with festive songs.

12:30pm. I was all set to see my two boys. I was so excited and scared at the same time. I needed help not to cry. They were a half hour late. I almost thought they weren't coming. I had the nurse call because my heart was racing. They finally arrived. What a good-looking family. My husband with the two boys. Oh, how my heart breaks. I was more broken that my husband wants to leave me. He bought me a nice Nike workout outfit for Christmas from the boys. I gave Jonathan chocolates and he left me one. That was so sweet. Jonathan and Louis looked amazing in their suits, bow ties, and cologne. My little men, looking sharp as always.

My dad called too. They bought Robert $600 cologne from Saks for Christmas and bought me nothing. I told him, "Why are you calling me?" He said, "To see how you're doing." I said, "Not good" and I hung up. I expected nothing from them. They rejected me way before I rejected them when they took my ex-husband's side. Feeling rejected hurts. I wanted to be separated from my husband in hopes he would make it work. Well. that plan backfired. Lord, was I wrong for what I did? Because I hate the consequences to setting boundaries. Being passive would have been just as painful, I must admit.

Virginia tried calling me but I just hung up on her. She takes no responsibility for her actions. She stuck to the lie that I told her not to come. I remember clearly- I said, "I am going to be released next week." That doesn't mean don't come. We had this discussion last time as well. She likes to make people believe what she wants to do something nice for you, but never follows through. She is an intentional liar. At least stir up a new fabricated story where we could have a different debate.

I didn't realize I gave the hospital permission to get Child Protective Services (CPS) involved. The hospital told me it was standard protocol. I didn't know I had an option to refuse it. I know we are both very good parents. I just left CPS a Merry Christmas voicemail and let them know that my husband has allowed me to speak to my children only twice a week. I did get to see them for Christmas. I couldn't comprehend why CPS got involved.

I need to fast from 5pm to 5pm. Help me Lord to put my trust in you alone. Give me self-control as I fast. I needed to find a shelter. 9:45pm Louis called me. I was so excited. They had a fabulous Christmas. Jonathan was out cold sleeping. I couldn't speak to him. I was so jealous that my sister-in-law gets to be with my children while I was trapped in a hospital. Oh Lord, my days here are almost over. Louis told me his school play wasn't until February. Thank you Lord that I will be able to go to his Charlie Brown play. I had three more days before release. I also had to find a personal injury attorney for my car accident.

11:15am Group Time-   Stephanie was scrapbooking inspiration for the present and future. I found a Cosmopolitan article from 2012. The article about Jake seemed too smart for me to entertain. I thought Jake's real alias was Rick. I don't think it's my ex-boyfriend Rick but it was fun imagining it.

My mom came to see me but I declined her visit. I requested my phone charger and my notebook and she didn't drop off either one. She dropped off Starbucks and food. My dad was pissed off that I declined my mother's visit. I explained to my dad, "How does it feel not to see your own child? You have kept me from seeing my kids by placing me here. I hope you understand now where I'm coming from."

Saturday 12/26/25 I had to go to the precinct and check whether they would escort me to my house to collect my belongings. I left my attorney a message, "Why is it that my husband has a pro bono attorney and I get kicked out of my house when my name is on the deed? I also don't understand how he got an order of protection effective immediately. When I requested an order of protection, I was made to wait." Raquel informed me that since I escaped from the hospital, everything became effective immediately. I ruined it for myself. She also informed me that Robert got my letter. She said he also received the post-nuptial papers to stay married. I was hoping to get that post-nuptial agreement refunded. I was so confused. *Did Robert consider the post-nuptial?*

12/27/15. Poor Jessy slurs her words because of the medication. She says it took her 45 minutes to get dressed. She can't find her bras. She constantly complains that they need to lower the medication. If she is still slurring, I would assume they haven't changed her medication. Jessy couldn't even walk. I suggested a wheelchair. She said, "No way." Another girl in our facility would pee in her pants and drool. Glendy threw up in our sink again. I had to throw out my toothbrush just in case. You never know how far vomit can splatter. Jessy asked the nurse, "Can the medication sometimes make you slow? The nurse said, "Yes, it is a side effect."

I needed to check with Brian Wellington, Esq as to how the order of protection can be removed. Robert told Raquel he doesn't want a divorce. He just wanted me on medication. What did he think medication will do? Robert sounded just like my parents. What will this magic pill turn me into? How about the Queen of England? With all her struggles, do you think a pill will fix everything?

11:15am. In rehab, I shared how I was worried about my believing I got worse once I'm released from the hospital because I want to get box braids. I want to dress like a cowgirl. I want to dress artsy with socks up to my knees and combat boots. Then I also enjoy dressing in my business attire. Glendy shared that she wants to be stronger. She is too sensitive and wants to grow a set of balls. I said, if that were possible, she could get with me. Everyone laughed. Janet said, we were both out of line. Without rehab life is too serious here. Janet said, "Glendy you need to go to church and get baptized." Glendy said, "I did already." Janet said, "You need to be baptized more than once." Ciara said, "Your husband is gay just for putting an order of protection against you. Or is he cheating? Because a man doesn't leave a wife unless he has someone else." I wouldn't be surprised by any of those assumptions.

12:00pm. Glendy was teaching Natalie a song. So funny. Jessy was cracking up and spilled water all over herself. I told her to try not to pee on herself. Must be the medication. She was slurping her soup out of the bowl. I was beginning to get worried about her. She said the spoon takes too long. I would have to agree.

My sister Raquel continued to defend my mother's actions. Everyone thinks they know best what medical treatment I should be receiving. Meanwhile, they were making my situation worse. Raquel blamed me for closing my business and divorcing my husband all at once. She explained this alarmed them, causing them to get involved. Is that how they justified their actions? I never wanted them to interfere. I don't remember asking them to help me. Raquel said she knew Robert was no good for me since day one. Regardless, that's for me to determine. No one else. I was never fond of her one-sided, opinionated husband who can never be corrected. If she can tolerate that persona, good for her. That's her life.

Aziz came to my rescue and drove me to a motel once I was released. He didn't stay with me because I was technically still married and he didn't want to be disrespectful in any way. His father had just passed away. He was struggling with his own grief and taking medication to mend his broken heart. We had not seen each other in over twenty-five years. A month before I was admitted into the mental health facility, my mother had seen Aziz when he dropped by the Wig Boutique to say hello and conveyed the news of his father's passing. I wasn't working that day. I found it to be such a coincidence because I was recently wondering how life was treating him. My mother confirmed that he was still living with his mother and they had sold their deli business. In Palestinian culture, the son lives with his parents. Even though he was born and raised in Venezuela, he never strayed from his values. Sometimes, you wonder what your life would have looked like if you took another path. Apparently, not much had changed for him. I had no regrets. I believe we were able to help each other get through our worst hurdles. Occasionally, he would check on me to make sure I was okay. I would do the same for him.

Erica came to the motel I was temporarily living at. I was awaiting a shelter to become available at The Safe Center. The sexual banging next door was obnoxious. The television from the next door at 4am also kept me up at night. I had to call the front desk to have them lower the noise. I was living a horrible nightmare I couldn't wake up from. The next day, The Safe Center contacted me saying that they had a room available in Brooklyn. I was so blessed Erica came to my rescue, and offered to host me for a few days to live with her and her husband instead. I hardly knew Erica. I had met her on the Lego line at the Roosevelt Field Mall and we became friends. God usually employs the people you would least expect to help you through your toughest times; even strangers.

I tried to rent a car but my license had expired. I wanted a Volkswagen Beetle Convertible but it was unavailable. The Lord knows I love Convertibles. I renewed my license and the next day, the soft-top Beetle became available. An Enterprise agent picked me up in front of Erica's house. I didn't have high expectations, which is my coping mechanism to avoid disappointments. Lord, you are so precious to me. I couldn't wait to blast the music in the car. God's timing is always better than ours. Delay is not denial. Guess what else? At 12:30pm, I scheduled an appointment with my gynecologist and had my IUD removed. What a relief. No more chronic yeast infections. When I told my gynecologist about my experience at Zucker Hillside hospital she said, "You should write a book." I responded facetiously, "Well, it's in the making." I left her office so elated to know my story is worth writing. Psychiatric Savior, I may call it. My savior Jesus will direct my footsteps when this book gets published one day. Lord, "I'm thinking bigger. Perhaps an Oscar-winning movie afterwards. No major expectations, of course. Just hopeful."

I went back to the Andrew Hotel and my belongings were still there along with some cash. Prior to my car accident, I had gone with my husband to view a convertible mini cooper to zip around in. I was too practical, so I told myself to hold off. I missed my Volvo Convertible C70 from my single years. This rent-a-car will do for now, until my finances are restored.

I drove the Volkswagen off the parking lot and got ready to feel alive outside of my prison walls. As I was driving to the salon for my hair appointment, I got rear ended from the back. I was thinking, what else can possibly happen to me?

Erica told me, "Use my chiropractor and he can put a claim through your insurance." I contacted her personal injury attorney. Too bad the chiropractor was in a committed relationship. I couldn't wait to visit him every two weeks. Now I have a massage therapist, acupuncturist, and a handsome doctor. Who can complain? These are the small luxuries of life we take for granted. This second car accident afforded me $10,000 to give to my divorce lawyer.

CHAPTER ELEVEN

UNFORESEEN POST TRAUMATIC STRESS DISORDER FINALLY SETTLED IN ONCE MY LIFE WASN'T FUELED BY MY ADRENALINE.

My mother and I made amends. When I was no longer on the run and safe back at my parents' home, I experienced Post-Traumatic Stress Disorder (PTSD). I felt like the battle was over and the adrenaline that I was fueled by had worn off. I experienced the overwhelming after-effects. I didn't want to leave my bed. I felt paralyzed. I had no house, no children, no job. Wig Boutique closed after 15 successful years. What purpose did I have in life now? I suffered like Job in the Bible. Job lost all his possessions, his health, his home, his seven sons and three daughters, and even his will to live. Job's friends were under the misconception that perhaps his tragic life was the consequence of his own sin. But in Job 1:8, God recognizes Job as, "blameless and upright, a man who fears God and shuns evil." Yes, bad things happen to good people. Job 1:6-12, Satan and the angels came before God, believing that if Job were struck with everything he possessed, he would surely curse God to his face. God gave Satan permission to test the faith of his son Job under one condition- you can strike Job with everything, but you cannot lay a finger on him. Satan is limited in what he can do and still needs permission from the Lord. Revelations 12:9 says, "that ancient serpent called the devil, or Satan, who leads the whole world astray. He was hurled to the earth, and his angels with him." I constantly make a conscious effort to recognize my savior and not be shaken by spiritual warfare that unfolds here on earth. I know this isn't about what my family did or about what my ex-husband did. This is the enemy using our loved ones to work against us and thus, divide us. If this is my test in life, I will not fall for the devil's schemes.

Job 1:18-20, Job discovered, "his sons and daughters were feasting and drinking wine at the oldest brother's house, when suddenly a mighty wind swept in from the desert and struck the four corners of the house. It collapsed on them and they were dead, and I am the only one who has escaped to tell you!" Jobs' first response was to fall to the ground in worship. He suffered great pain. Job had wished he had never been born in Job 3:1. In my worship of pain, I cry and beg for relief and comfort because I know I can't get rid of my pain without the Lord's gentle love. I experienced the spiritual warfare that exists but I also feel the Lord's protection over my life, which comforts me. When I ask the Lord to fight my battles, I just need to be still as promised in Exodus 14:14.

This time, Job is afflicted with horrible skin sores. Job 2:9 says, His wife encourages him to curse God, which would be exactly what Satan was looking for. Job's wife even suggested Job give up and die, but Job refused. Job painfully accepted his circumstances. Job never understood why he was being afflicted. He questioned God many times just like we all do. In Job 10:15, "If I am guilty-woe to me! Even if I am innocent, I cannot lift my head, for I am full of shame and drowned in my afflictions." Job just kept praising the Lord and trusting God no matter what. Job 42:10, "the Lord made him prosperous again and gave him twice as much as he had before." I just remind myself that God will restore my life the way he did for Job. This is a temporary test. I know my outcome will be better than before. I refuse to allow my emotions to dictate my life. I constantly remind myself that feelings are not facts.

CHAPTER TWELVE

CELEBRATED MY 40TH BIRTHDAY PARTY A YEAR LATER WITH MY TWELVE DISCIPLES AT THE SUPPER CLUB IN NEW YORK CITY.

I invited my frenemy Carolina to my 40th birthday party. I forgave her and her husband for admitting me into the hospital. She was my Judas. Marika, who didn't extend her shelter to me either, was also invited on my party bus. Both Marika and Carolina became my ex-husband's best friends after my birthday celebration. Marika loved bringing Robert her famous rice pudding on the holidays after our divorce. I just found the whole situation weird. She was married with two girls and one boy. Ironically, Carolina wasn't fond of my ex-husband when we were married. She had temporarily stopped being my friend for a while because Robert was rude to her husband Paul. I was scratching my head. *Now she's best friends with him after my divorce.*

Robert was neurotic and her husband didn't understand that. Meanwhile, Carolina is also quite particular with order. Paul took the liberty to go into our freezer and started the BBQ. Since it started to rain Robert didn't want to BBQ or clean the grill. This wasn't communicated and my husband must have made Paul uncomfortable. I understood both Paul and Robert's emotions. I apologized that my husband was rude, but I needed Carolina to also understand Robert didn't want to clean the grill. Yet Carolina herself was overly disturbed when things were not in order. It was strange that she couldn't empathize reflecting from her own neuroticism. I reminded Carolina of the time she had a playdate and was putting all the toys away because she couldn't deal with a mess. I felt uncomfortable that my kids couldn't touch anything despite being invited on a playdate. That doesn't mean we have to stop being friends. Most people can't see their own reflection when it's not appealing. The Bible says in Matthew 7:3, "Why do you look at the speck of sawdust in your brother's eye and pay no attention to the plank in your own eye?"

Carolina never spoke to me again after my 40th birthday and became best friends with my ex-husband. She visited Robert during our separation and was doing homework with my children. She also attended the birthday parties he was hosting instead of mine.

This Luxury party bus didn't even feel like my birthday outing. I had several *friends of a friend* attend. The bus could accommodate twenty-four people comfortably. Ironically, I had my twelve disciples with me. Maryann, whom I barely knew, started changing the radio station to rock music, which I don't particularly listen to. My other girlfriend, Lori and her spouse, were smoking weed in the front of the limo bus, which I don't do. I was thinking to myself, *What is going on?* Toward the end of the night, Claudia, another friend of a friend, requested that she get dropped off in front of her house. Meanwhile, I paid the driver to pick up and drop off from my house to save on time and enjoy the night in NYC. The driver stated that he will only follow my instructions. I suppose Claudia was persuasive enough to have the driver drop her off in front of her house. A chain reaction transpired. Another girl wanted to get dropped off in front of her house while I was being charged per hour. So, I told Claudia that

I didn't appreciate her redirecting the driver when she wasn't paying him. She responded curtly as though to say, *who cares.* She mistook my kindness for weakness. I cannot accept that. I sternly told her, "What are you, a fucking princess to get front door service?"

All my so-called friends labeled me bipolar after my altercation. My friends were not accustomed to me standing up for myself, especially using vulgar words. Okay, I didn't have to use the F-bomb word. I just didn't know what language she would understand. They preferred the old Ava that was a quiet people pleaser. If addressing people is the same as being bipolar, then I suppose I'll own the name. The old Ava, the one who existed before her escapade with the psychiatric facility, doesn't exist anymore. In all reality, I probably didn't even speak to her as strongly as I should have. I was still ignored.

Claudia was inviting her husband onto the limousine bus to introduce himself to everyone. Her dog entered the bus as well. It was a family reunion here. She asked if anyone wanted to use the restroom delaying us from getting home. Meanwhile, we have a private restroom. I kept telling myself, I earn $10 an hour and I spent $1,000 to have a special 40th birthday that was already deferred by a year. This was going down as another birthday disaster. I blew out the candles and silently said to myself, *Goodbye 40. Hello 41.* Time to get a whole new group of friends.

I was at a complete stop, waiting for the traffic light to turn green at 8:45am, while commuting to Elizabeth Arden Red Door Spa in Garden City. All of a sudden, I look in my rear-view mirror and I witness the car behind me collide right into me. This caused a domino effect, as I collided into the car halted ahead of me. Me and this poor Honda Pilot have taken a beating in the past few months. The car was completely totaled. My car insurance gave me the book value of the vehicle. I was still able to drive the Honda Pilot with a salvaged title. My vehicle and I were both broken and still persevering. I was back at the chiropractor's office, personal injury attorney, and acupuncture specialist. I desperately needed the chiropractor's assistance and the acupuncture services as life continued to drown me in stress and my body formed several knots in its defense. These three accidents were a blessing in disguise to get me out of a bad marriage and afford my attorney. I was able to sell my engagement ring for $6k and my parents gave each of us $10k for Christmas. That $10k gift went directly to my lawyer. I wish I could have used it towards a newer car. I had a garage sale and sold everything, including the bathroom vanity. Little by little, I would start over with everything new. I knew I would rebuild my life again but this time smarter and better.

I had to rent a vehicle while my car was under repair. I inquired about a convertible again. The Rent-A-Car agent told me she had a BMW Convertible. I was so elated. God knows how to elevate my life. I paid the difference of what my insurance allotted me. I was reminded of my single days when I drove around a Volvo Convertible paid in full. Traveling to Paris, Ireland, Spain, London, Amsterdam, Venice, Egypt, and Italy was recreational for me. Once I got married, I had to downgrade my lifestyle. I wasn't able to sustain the two of us as I was the breadwinner. Thank you, Lord, for upgrading my vehicle, even if it is a temporary rental. This car accident afforded me another $10,000 to give to my divorce lawyer. It wasn't much, but it was better than nothing.

Around this time, a guy named Allen messaged me on Facebook messenger. Allen said, "I met you at your cousin's New Years party. I had taken the family picture of your boys with their cousins." Allen attended as my cousin Frank's guest. I explained to him, "I wasn't at the party. You may have had me mistaken for my cousin Isabelle. I spent my New Year's in a psychiatric facility." I was going through a divorce. I couldn't be bothered with anyone in my life at the moment. A few days later Allen saw me at a nightclub with Erica. He kept encouraging both me and Erica to dinner with him. I still refused. I didn't have the mindset for a relationship. All I really wanted to do was just sleep and never come out from underneath the covers. I had declined all of his invitations. Until one day, I realized I can't live in self pity forever. He knew my situation that I lost my house, my business and I was living at my parents' house. I felt like such a loser. Allen bought me a membership to the gym. We would meet there every day and then go swimming at LA Fitness. He took me to dinner every night. Occasionally, we would go to the foot spa. He was temporarily living with his mother because he was renovating his new home. Allen surprised me with an appointment to get my hair colored the night before my court appearance, so I could look my best. He was unbelievable.

Pampering myself wouldn't have even crossed my mind. Then he surprised me again and showed up at the hair salon appointment and brought me lunch. Never in my life was I bestowed with such Royal treatment. There were days I couldn't snap out of my sadness. I told Allen I didn't know how to interact with my children. I felt so estranged from my boys and paralyzed to even be able to cook or entertain them. I just couldn't believe everything had been taken from me, my home, my children, and my dignity.

On the day I was scheduled to visit my kids, Allen surprised me with bazooka water Nerf guns. He would buy me gift cards to iHop and fast-food restaurants so I could enjoy some quality time with my children. One day he got me a membership at the RPM raceway. The boys and I raced high speed electric go-karts. I found it difficult to introduce my kids to Allen. I didn't want to acclimate my boys to another man. Not yet, anyway. It seemed like an inappropriate step, unless I were engaged to someone. Why create more confusion in their lives? It was probably hard enough that their parents were separated. Allen was very understanding and never pushed the issue. That didn't stop Allen from still buying a mini-iPad for me to give them as a gift for no special occasion. He also gave me a Hoverboard and Beats headphones that I could gift them. My boys just assumed it was from their mom. My husband Robert was furious, "I thought you didn't have any money?" I had to explain, "I'm dating someone." More injury to this ugly divorce because I'm not intentionally trying to hurt anyone or get revenge. Romans 12:19 says, "Do not take revenge, my friends, but leave room for God's wrath, for it is written: "It is mine to avenge; I will repay, says the Lord."

Robert asked my cousin Edwin about Allen's background. Robert's words to me were, "Ava, he seems like a nice guy, but I would rather see you with a lawyer." My heart melted because I never set such high standards for myself. I was a very simple-minded person with no inkling of my worth. For the first time, I heard Robert tell me my values need to be higher because I am deserving. I just wish I believed that for myself. I will never forget these words. To hear this for the first time was so powerful to me. Especially coming from the man I was about to divorce.

Allen never stopped surprising me. One time, he gave me a gift card for the supermarket. I didn't even need it, as I had the Supplemental Nutrition Assistance Program (SNAP) card. Allen took me to the Smithsonian Museum in NYC. We ate at the Hard Rock Cafe and then watched a Broadway Show afterwards. I have never dated anyone more generous than him. I was usually the one giving to others. In Acts 20:35 it says, "It is more blessed to give than to receive." Receiving was something that made me very uncomfortable.

Deep inside, I wasn't comfortable being in this relationship with Allen. We dated for four months. Allen's daughter was vaping in middle school. His other daughter got her belly button pierced. We went to dinner one night and his daughter ate the steak with her fingers. "They were not taught to eat with utensils?" I lost my appetite at that moment. Outside the restaurant, she disposed of her empty water bottle in the street. She told me not to tell, as if I'm okay with that. Yikes, I'm not looking to be a wicked stepmom and admonish her. Nor do I want my children to be exposed to this kind of environment. One morning I went with Allen to the courthouse because he was enforcing an order of protection against his daughter's baby daddy. I only thought this takes place on Jerry Springer but now it was creeping into my life. I could not escape this reality show. I just need them to stop filming. Allen is a great father, but there was no structure or discipline here. I felt sad for Allen's daughters as they lacked proper guidance or etiquette. I just don't envision myself starting over with someone else's family. I want my children back and my life back. I didn't know how to break off the relationship with Allen. I didn't want him to feel like he was taken for granted. I had to find a way to repay him for all he has done for me. I was able to save $500. I slipped it in his back pocket. I know it wasn't much, but if I had more, I would have given it to him. He felt me slip the money in his back pocket and immediately he asked, "What is this? Break up money?" *Wow, how did he know?* I didn't even have to say it. I had to be completely honest with Allen. I told him I wanted to reconcile with my husband. Allen took the money from his back pocket and threw it back into my car. He said, "I'm never taking money from you."

I was crying to the Lord because I wanted to return to my husband because I didn't enjoy dating another man and breaking bread with someone else's children. I was attending Allen's grand children's birthday parties with his ex-wife and the whole situation felt so estranged. I cried to Robert to try to restore our marriage. Robert was acting as if I was the one who went outside of the marriage and there is nothing to restore. Technically, I wasn't officially divorced so I did commit adultery. Just because I served Robert the papers, it doesn't justify my actions to be involved with anyone else. Robert began acting as though I initially defiled him. I remembered 1 Samuel 6:6, "Why do you harden your hearts as the Egyptians and Pharaoh did? When he treated them harshly, did they not send the Israelites out so they could go on their way?" I think Robert forgot I left because I was being mistreated. I have to forgive him too. I'm asking for a clean start. I'll forgive you; you forgive me. Allen called Robert and explained to him that I wanted to reconcile. I couldn't believe that Allen was truly looking out for my best interests even if it meant our relationship would come to an end.

Trying to start over with someone I hardly knew was painful. I didn't want to leave my comfort zone as I had so many years already invested in my spouse. Allen was a saint in my life and played a big part of my recovery. Finally, after shedding so many tears, the Lord must have said, "Okay have it your way Ava, I can't see you cry like this." All of a sudden, my ex-husband's heart softened and we went on two dates. I thought things were getting better until he decided to sleep out. He stated he would stay at his sister's house. Another time, he told me he had to take care of his sister's dogs. *Oh Lord! What did I pray for?* Now I pray for your will God, not mine. I don't know what's best for me. I just know I wanted the pain to go away.

At least in my heart, I obeyed the scripture to try to reconcile the marriage as stated in, 1 Corinthians 7:10-11, "To the married I give this charge (not I, but the Lord): the wife should not separate from her husband. But if she does, she should remain unmarried or else be reconciled to her husband, and the husband should not divorce his wife." I believe the Lord released me from the marriage because in 1 Corinthians 7:15 says, "if the unbelieving partner leaves, let it be so. In such cases the brother or sister is not enslaved. God has called you to peace." Robert was not looking to reconcile, therefore he left me. Robert was looking to live a double life while banking on my financial security.

Allen threw $200 in my car, because he knew I wouldn't take it. He wanted me to obtain Robert's court records to prove he possessed drugs in his workplace while we were married. I had to bail him out of that as well. I took our tax money, which I had recently received to pay the bails bondsman and attorney. Perhaps I can prove Robert to be an unfit father to raise our children just as he depicted me as suffering from a mental illness. I printed out his records and gave it to my divorce lawyer. It didn't faze her and she didn't bring it up in court. In life I always felt overlooked, so this was nothing unusual for me.

I found the strength to rebuild my life again with the help of Allen's friendship. Shortly after, I got a job at Elizabeth Arden Red Door in Garden City, NY. I used to be a nail technician in my college years earning amazing gratuity, which helped me pay off my tuition. I never imagined I would return to this high school trade. Luckily, I always renewed my cosmetology license. Occasionally, I would get a $50 tip here and there. Here I am earning $10 an hour while paying a babysitter. This didn't make much financial sense at the time. It's bad enough I had limited time with my boys and now I couldn't even see them. My previous babysitter accepted a daily fee from me as opposed to her previous substantial salary. After a few weeks working at the salon, I was able to get the days I needed so my job did not interfere with my visitation. I'm so glad I made the sacrifice and refused to quit. Proverbs 3:5-6 says, "Trust in the Lord with all your heart and lean not on your own understanding, in all your ways submit to him, and he will make your path straight." I was fortunate enough that a co-worker left and I was able to take over her hours that better aligned with my schedule. Within a few months, I was able to reopen Wig Boutique.

CHAPTER THIRTEEN

REMARRIED WIG BOUTIQUE AND DISCOVERED TRICHOMANIA AND BARIATRICS SUPPORT GROUPS.

I was blessed with an opportunity to remarry Wig Boutique and fall in love with my retail store all over again. After 15 years of business, it had become so routine and dull. I worked at the Red Door Spa until I was in a position to relaunch Wig Boutique with the help of my mother. I went to my local library to find an html programming book for dummies to redesign my website. The librarian recommended the Small Business Development Center (SBDC) at Farmingdale University. I thought I would be enrolling in a course. I didn't realize the SBDC is a free resource funded by the federal government to help small businesses within the United States to scale up. I met with the business consultant and she inspired me to write amazing flirty content and design my website more personable. I learned how to optimize my website for mobile devices using my GoDaddy account. I did my own Search Engine Optimization (SEO) and produced long and valuable content to generate keywords that drive traffic to my site. I learned to develop blog articles that would inspire others. It was like I fell in love with Wig Boutique all over again. I felt rejuvenated and stimulated every day as I worked on new marketing strategies. Rediscovering my latent capabilities and reinventing myself with new skills to grow my store allowed me to feel so accomplished.

Just when I thought I knew the wig business inside out, I discovered a new target market I never reached before. I learned about my customer's Trichotillomania Syndrome and I also discovered a Bariatric Support Group. Trichotillomania is hair pulling, skin picking and or nail biting used to self soothe the nervous system. These are habits that are not easy to break free from. Bariatric surgery facilitates weight loss, by sometimes causing hair loss as a side effect. This occurs because of the body's response to surgery, altered diet and quick weight loss. I feel so blessed to be able to deliver hair solutions for most women's challenging circumstances. I love makeovers because my life reflects that every single day. Changing my life, my hair and my wardrobe inspires me to wake up in the morning. I don't suffer from hair loss but on some days, I'm pretty disappointed with my appearance. When I wear a wig, all that changes. I am able to fake my confidence with my renewed appearance. I may be fake on the outside but I know I'm real on the inside.

One of my first blogs was, *I'm excited to share my new logo for Wig Boutique. The fonts I chose for promoting my business recognition reflect my journey as each letter has the swirls for adult coloring that helped me be artsy, colorful and creative while in the mental hospital. I wanted to set my retail store apart from others exactly like my logo, creative, calming and therapeutic experience.*

On Halloween day, I closed my doors at Wig Boutique after 15 years. It was sad to say Goodbye, in search of a new location. God's timing couldn't have been better. I had personal struggles. I had to take care of myself and I returned to the place where I had almost lost hope. Being thankful, I returned to the original location, but this time with a drive to be even more successful than before. Life is ever changing. Don't be left behind. I had to update my website, learn social media marketing and get current with technology. How intimidating, but I did it! With the help of the Small Business Development Center, Google reviews from my customers and social media marketing. I even learned how to blog. Many thanks to the help of Godaddy.com employees as well. I'm still doing what I love best. Helping people find their beauty. The lesson learned from all this is, we need to keep reinventing ourselves in order to grow and fall in love again with ourselves. Thank you all for visiting my store and keeping my business alive.

I never thought my skills from Hofstra University in the Business Computer Information Systems would come to good use. I chose this major because my oldest sister, Silvia, told me there was no money in art. I experimented with programming but I didn't enjoy it. I found myself isolated in a booth and dreaming code when I was sleeping. I used programming languages called C++, Java script, SQL and HTML. I would rather learn French or Italian, "Bonjour or Ciao." Opening Wig Boutique was me leveraging my creative talent and social outlet. Looking back, I see how God arranges the pieces together to make it all work. Even though I thought college was a waste of time, my education was beneficial.

After my time at the psychiatric facility, I broke free of many triggers. I developed a rugged alligator skin. I did have a customer mistake my radar. While at work, a customer bought a wig from me and we had a heartfelt conversation. She shared her personal life with me and I shared mine so she could find comfort in her situation. The next week she came back to the store with a different demeanor. Her personality and approach were completely different. She threw the wig box at me and said, "I don't want this wig." I politely replied, "I'm sorry but the sign clearly says, no returns and exchanges because of the health laws." Her response was, "Well I'll just call my credit card company and get my money back if you refuse to give me a refund." I blatantly told her, "I think that is a great idea. Take the wig because I can't resell it. You should get your money back because you obviously need it more than I do." I know in my heart she didn't come to return the wig. She was just looking for someone to fight with and I wasn't going to entertain her drama. She mistook my kindness for weakness. She left my store infuriated, screaming, "I'm going to call child protective services on you." She remembered the story I told her about my ugly divorce. I stayed quiet and just prayed for her in my head. She never called her credit card company for a refund because what she really wanted was a fight. I didn't let the enemy win this battle. The enemy will use anyone he can to try to make you stumble. James 4:7 "Submit yourselves therefore to God. Resist the devil and he will flee from you." She fled alright.

A year later, the same customer returned to Wig Boutique and I helped her as if I didn't remember who she was. She asked, "Did the other girl who worked here get fired?" not realizing I was the same person. I let her know, "She's not working today." She thanked me for being so helpful and made up stories about how the other girl was so rude to her. I just giggled in my mind and was thankful she didn't recognize me.

I saw a psychologist for my supposed bipolar disorder, since it was covered under my insurance. I wanted to prove that I was emotionally balanced in order to get my children back. I explained to the psychologist, "I had left the hospital because I was falsely accused of attempted suicide. My husband put me there because our marriage was falling apart. I was considering divorce and my ex-husband was scared I would get full custody of the children. My parents also conspired to put me in the hospital believing the alleged lies my ex-husband. My parents never confirmed if Robert was telling the truth because I was very private with my life. My mom disclosed to me that she didn't think I would share. She was correct. I wouldn't want to alarm them with my personal life." The psychologist immediately called my mother to verify my story. My mother confirmed our conversation.

The psychologist decided to prescribe Abilify medication. I told her, "I refused medication in the hospital so why would I take it now? I just needed a letter to validate I don't need medication. I'm holistic, and will organically get better. I exercise, I journal, I pray and I eat healthy. I believe in therapy, that is why I'm here, but not medicine." The psychologist explained that I speak fast and she has a hard time following my story. I explained, "I speak fast because our session is only 45 minutes. I'm trying to squeeze as much information into my story so you understand what challenges I have recently faced." I told her, "If you can't follow my story then interrupt me and let me know where you got lost."

I felt I explained my story properly. Obviously, I couldn't convince her. Nor does she know that most Spanish people talk fast and talk over each other and we understand each other just fine. The psychiatrist prescribed me 8 mg of Abilify (generic name is Aripiprazole). I told her that I would follow her instructions. I picked up the prescription at the pharmacy to pretend as though I was taking the medication to get my children back.

The following week, I went to see the psychologist again. She immediately wanted to increase my prescription to 10mg. I asked her, "Why are you increasing the dose so quickly? And what am I supposed to do with the previous prescription?" She explained, "The pharmacy will still fill the prescription because I'm providing a higher dose, so don't worry." This sounded like pharmaceutical sales and commission fraud to me. I asked her, "What should I do with the previous pills?" Her response, "Throw them out or cut them in halves." At that moment, I realized I was healed because I didn't go back to my previous sensitive self, into a ball of tears. Getting people to believe me used to be my trigger for a long time because I was molested. Identifying your trigger is the key to gradual healing. I told myself, *I know your games, Satan and it's okay if people don't believe me because I know my own truth and so does Jesus.*

One time, I told my cousin Isabelle my marriage was getting better and she said, "I don't believe you," and I began to cry. I didn't understand why her words hurt me so much. It was just her opinion. Isabelle said, "I'm family so I'm just telling you how it is." I told her, "Call my husband and ask him yourself." I wanted her to believe me. She called my husband to confirm. Looking back, Isabelle was dealing with her own marital problems and perhaps misery does love company. I'm sure she didn't want to feel alone in her dark world.

That night I got on my knees and asked the Lord, "Why am I crying over her opinion?" I know my own truth so this shouldn't hurt me. That night the Lord whispered, "She didn't believe you." Then I remembered how when I was older, I finally told my parents I was molested by my godfather. My dad acted surprised as if it were impossible for something like that to happen. *Wow, what a clear revelation, Lord.* I never knew my past had such an impact on my heart if not believed. As an adult, I was mature enough to understand my parents rather live in denial as a coping mechanism to hide from reality. I'm thankful, I no longer need people to affirm my truth but God alone. Digging deeper with the Lord to understand your own pain is so critical.

As a child, I had forgiven my abuser. I told myself, *perhaps my Godfather is repeating what was done to him.* I knew as a child we lived in a fallen world and life wasn't fair. I saw it all around me. My parents exposed me to people who were less fortunate and others who were from affluent backgrounds. I have cousins who speak slang and cousins who articulate their words precisely because of their environment. I'm thankful my humble parents acclimated me to both conditions. I feel comfortable in both situations.

CHAPTER FOURTEEN

HOW MANY JUDGES MUST YOU SEE BEFORE A DECISION IS FINALIZED? DOES THIS EVER END?

Who wants to be bounced from courtroom to courtroom? What started in the Supreme Court, went to Trial, then Family Court, then Appellate Court and back where we started- in the Supreme Court. The baton was practically thrown from one person to another, recklessly. Court houses are so intimidating and anxiety-inducing because we don't know what the outcome will be. Nor do you want to say anything that may sound incriminating. I had to take a deep breath and say, "God, you appointed Aron in the Bible to be Moses' speaker because Moses was too scared. I too am petrified. Lord, give me the comfort that my lawyer will be my effective speaker like Aron in the Bible." I had to take another deep breath and ask, "Lord, give me the staff you gave Moses because I'm terrified to speak." In Exodus 4:10, Moses said to the Lord, "O Lord, I have never been eloquent, neither in the past nor since you have spoken to your servant. I am slow of speech and tongue." That's exactly how I was feeling.

My sister Silvia would always correct my speech because some of my pronunciations were off. I didn't mind being corrected, but she exercised it in a demeaning manner. Public speaking wasn't my strength. Especially, as a victim of sexual abuse, I muzzled my mouth. God reassured Moses that he would help him speak and teach Moses what to say. But Moses pleaded with God to still send someone else to speak in Exodus 4:12. I was grateful to have my lawyer speak on my behalf. I needed my invisible staff to reassure myself of God's miracle touch that he passed on to Moses to be believed.

I called my 9-year-old son Louis from the courthouse and said, "Please pray for me." He tells me, "Mom, I don't have to, you are wearing your Armor of Christ." I wanted to cry because this child of mine is so amazing. He captures and retains what I teach him. How we need to wear our full armor of God so we can stand against the devil's schemes. The armor in Ephesians 6:14-17 consists of, "the belt of truth buckled around your waist, with the breastplate of righteousness in place, and with your feet fitted with the readiness that comes from the gospel of peace. In addition to all this, take up the shield of faith, with which you can extinguish all the flaming arrows of the evil one. Take the helmet of salvation and the word of the Spirit, which is the word of God." I had my invisible belt, breastplate, boots, shield and helmet on and I didn't even know it. God promises in Isaiah 54:17, "No weapon formed against me shall prosper, and every tongue which rises against me God shall condemn." This sounds all so powerful but I was still intimidated in court. Sometimes, I forget I have my invisible armor on. It was pertinent for me to meditate and remind myself no weapon formed against me shall prosper. Fear is not from God.

During break time at the Supreme Court, I went to the diner with my dad because my ex-husband was using my family to testify as witnesses. My dad told me, "Ava, you love yourself too much." I said, "How so?" He said, "Because you exercise, you put on your makeup every day, and you make sure you look good." I never thought that was a signifier of how much I love myself. I thought the best revenge is to look your best so they can't see how broken you are. My father's words will never leave my heart. Self-care is self-love and I didn't even realize. There were so many things I accomplished but didn't give myself enough credit for.

Thankfully, I have strangers that remind me how beautiful I am. Recently, as I was boarding the plane, a flight attendant said I looked familiar and asked if I was famous. I love women who know how to love other women with affirmation, because how I truly feel inside doesn't reflect my outside. It's so refreshing how the Lord wants to remind me this through others until I truly believe it for myself. I'm just a work in progress. My favorite compliment is when I'm told I look like Eva Mendez. Occasionally, I get Paula Abdul. I wanted to tell the flight attendant I'm famous in God's eyes because he knew my name even before I was born, Isaiah 43:1-7. When I was asked what I liked most about my physical appearance, I felt stumped. I had a

> YOU DESERVE TO NOTICE YOURSELF WITH AMAZING FEATURES. WHAT ARE THREE ATTRIBUTES YOU LOVE ABOUT YOUR PHYSICAL APPEARANCE?

friend help me distinguish myself with my eyes, hips and lips. Meanwhile, I don't care for my hips. But she made me realize I like my waist line.

My best friend from high school, Virginia, always puts me on a pedestal and reminds me of my accomplishments. Even though I Graduated from Hofstra University with a BA in Business Computer Information Systems, founded and incorporated Wig

Boutique Ltd., designed my own website, bought my first home while single, taught myself social media marketing and still didn't see my own self-worth.

Living paycheck-to-paycheck was not my idea of success. Success to me meant being debt free. Paying off my home was | HOW WOULD YOU DEFINE SUCCESS? | more important than material things. According to Proverbs 22:7, "The borrower is servant to the lender." We lived paycheck to paycheck, because I didn't marry a man who had much to contribute economically, nor had a college degree, or trade school experience. When I pass away, I plan to leave my real estate to my children but also my future grandchildren as part of my success. My goal is Proverbs 12:33, "A good man leaves an inheritance to his children's children." Today success to me means maintaining my joy, even during chaos and financial struggles. There is nothing more powerful than being optimistic of your emotions in all circumstances. God's purpose is greater even when we don't understand it.

After Virginia's shared her reflection of me, I started to see myself as an accomplished woman. My son Luke once told me, "Mommy if you ever divorce daddy, I'm going with you because you are good with the finances." I just laughed. Even my son, when he was just 4 years old, recognized my achievements. Sometimes it takes that one certain person's opinion to finally register how valuable you are.

I had specifically told God that I'm in love with him alone, but if he wanted to send me a good man, I would promise to be celibate till marriage. Not that I was a virgin, just a recycled one. I requested that my future husband have green eyes, is Spanish and looks European. When I first met my husband in church, his nickname was Gringo.

WHAT ARE YOU MOSTLY RECOGNIZED FOR BY OTHERS? BE OPEN TO ASK YOUR FRIENDS WHAT ATTRIBUTE DO THEY LIKE MOST ABOUT YOU AND START BELIEVING IT FOR YOURSELF.

This Spanish term means white boy, because he didn't look Hispanic. He was Colombian with green eyes. Who knew you could be that specific with the Lord. Later in life, I learned you have to pray bigger because when you ask for little, you get little. When you pray for big you get big. So please readers, you're worth it. Don't make the same mistake I made. The Lord wants to spoil you but you have to believe

MAKE A CONSCIENCE EFFORT TO THINK OF THREE THINGS YOU ARE THANKFUL FOR TODAY AND THE NEAR FUTURE.

you're worth it. The Bible says in Matthew 21:22, "And whatever you ask in prayer, you will receive, if you have faith." I give thanks even before I receive my blessings because the Bible also says in Mark 11:24, "Therefore I tell you, whatever you ask in prayer, believe that you have received it, and it will be yours." God can do the impossible so why pray for little when God's word promises to give you so much more if you trust him. I'm also thankful for the unanswered prayers. Not everything we ask for will benefit us.

I had pleaded with my ex-husband to take $45K and accept joint custody of the children. I told him, "I would rather give you the money to go towards our children than to spend it on the lawyer." But he turned down my offer. He also didn't want to share the children 50/50. Either he wanted to see me go broke or he thought he was going to get more money out of this divorce with both the house and kids. I told Robert he could continue living in the house and I would start from scratch again. He refused my request. The $45k went to my divorce lawyer instead and so much more money went on my various credit cards. My business sense told me to use my JetBlue credit card for frequent-flyer points. At least my financial debt will reward me in the long term. I may be broke, but I can still soar and fly high with JetBlue. I could use a vacation when this is all over. Seeing the positive in all these dark places is what allowed me to persevere. My other credit cards allowed me to redeem my points for gift cards so I could give generous Christmas presents. I was just thankful to still be able to give when I really didn't have anything. I never stopped tithing, which means setting aside a certain amount of one's income for God. Tithing refers to a tenth of one's income because the word literally means tenth. Tithing is rooted from the Biblical story of Abraham presenting a tenth of the war spoils to Melchizedek, the king of Salem. In the Old Testament, Jews brought 10% of their harvest to a storehouse as a welfare plan for the needy or in case of famine. 2 Corinthians 9:7 says, "Each of you should give what you have decided in your heart to give, not reluctantly or under compulsion, for God loves a cheerful giver." I believe this is why I am never without.

I moved back to my mother's house after a year of hiding at Erica's house. My parents had begged me to return home. Once I returned, my mother started slipping the 8 mg of Abilify medication in my tea at night without my knowledge. The Judge asked me and Robert to cohabitate every other week so the children are not uprooted from their home. Upon this, my mother informed me she slipped the medication in my tea at night, since she was worried about medication withdrawal. I wasn't thrilled she did that, but getting upset wasn't going to change the circumstances. My goodness. Here we go again. My mother thinks she is helping me. I told myself it's just 8mg. Probably 8mg is as effective as a placebo pill. In life, I've learned that the only person you can trust is God. I keep my expectations low when it comes to people and my hopes high with Christ. I requested the Holy Spirit to help me maintain my trust in the Lord more than ever before. Relinquishing my control to God is not easy. Occasionally, doubt creeps in.

My ex-husband hired a forensic therapist as directed by the courts. The forensic therapist, Mr. Vizio had us meet him at his office and take this extensive questionnaire to understand our personality patterns. Mr. Vizio then made a house visit to Robert's dad and then my mother's house to investigate the case. My mother told Mr. Vizio that I was not taking my medication and I was doing well without it. She thought she was helping me once again. My mother knew I kept picking up my prescriptions from CVS pharmacy so why in the heck would she tell him that. He was hired by my ex-husband for his own benefit. My mother's actions contributed to my loss of custody. My other stumbling block was the wicked Law Guardian. I wrote a letter to the Director of the Law Guardian, to have her removed from the case and replaced with someone else.

August 14, 2019

Att: James Robinson, Director of Law Guardian Programs

I would like to file a complaint against Rebecca Smith Law Guardian to Louis Martinez, born 05/21/07 and Jonathan Martinez, born 07/15/09. My Divorce Decree was finalized February 2017. My children were requested to be in therapy by Judge Cornell in the Supreme Court as of that date. It is now August 2019 and I have been to Family Court numerous times trying to have my visitations enforced as he will not allow a therapist for my children. I finally found a therapist for the Children as Judge Thomson in Nassau County Family Court has requested to move this case forward.

Attached please see emails correspondence I have sent that are disturbing to me. No mom should be taken away from her children. The Law Guardian, Rebecca Smith has put the roadblock to enforce family unity. I see my children one day a week with designated supervision by my parents. My ex-husband has denied me supervision because he got into a disagreement with my father. I told Rebecca Smith I'm in court because he needs to assign another supervisor. Her response was, "You know he won't do that!" She knows he is blocking me from seeing the children and she continues to favor Robert Martinez's actions. I had my father come to court to enforce supervision once again. This is a biased situation that needs to be addressed. She is in complete denial that my ex-husband is hurting me because I left his abusive ways and now he is trying to hurt me using my children as bait. The law guardian has spoken to me in a harsh tone of voice that I am not to contact her. Meanwhile, it was my lawyer who advised me to speak to her while I was in the Supreme Court. I apologized to Rebecca Smith not knowing I am not warranted to speak to her. Yet she accepted Robert Martinez's conversations to brainwash her thoughts to keep me away from my children.

It has now been 4 years without my children. My ex-husband has made false (CPS) Unfounded Child Protective Services allegations against me and an order of protection for me to stay away from my children since November 2015. Rebecca Smith fails to see any of this. Rebecca Smith also stated the kids don't want to see me because I only gave them socks for Christmas. Meanwhile, I bought my son Northface gloves, North Face boots and socks for Christmas. What I purchase for my children has no reflection on who I am as a mother. The socks were a personal jest between my son and I because my ex-husband stated I never bought them anything, not even a pair of socks. I pay child support and when I'm with my children I pay for the movies, dinners and their clothing for school. The law guardian is inappropriate to believe everything my ex-husband communicates to her. I need your help in this matter as I don't know what else to do. Nor do I want this conduct to happen to another mother in the future. Please have this matter addressed.

I only pray I can have her removed from my next court date August 21st.

Sincerely, Ava Martinez

September 24, 2019

Att: James Robinson

Re: Complaint against Rebecca Smith, Esq.

Martinez vs. Martinez

I am requesting you contact my family therapist Dr. Johnson to discuss the awkward conversation he had with Rebecca Smith. Rebecca Smith was disturbed by his Christian faith and was asking him to review my medical records which have nothing to do with the children. Her efforts to taint my image is definitely inappropriate and his faith shouldn't be a concern to her. I have signed the waiver for you to speak to Dr. Johnson directly to prove her conduct is biased on this matter and I hope the appropriate action will be taken.

Sincerely, Ava Martinez

No investigation was undertaken in reference to the unjust law guardian. My therapist provided me with a letter to give to the Judge in defense of the Law Guardians actions.

February 29, 2020

Dear Hon. Maria S. Cornell:

Re: Ava Martinez

The above named patient has been seeing me for therapeutic services commencing June 12, 2019 and continues bi-weekly. She has been joined by her two sons Louis and Jonathan. The purpose for the visits was to facilitate healthy communications between herself and her sons with whom she has visitation, but who live with their father.

Although there were sessions in therapy that seemed to bring them together, there were sessions in which the boys, especially Louis, manifested resistance and a non-compliant spirit. That spirit even showed itself in Louis's response to me that "he does not like me." This response came as a result of my having to speak candidly about displayed behaviors in session that were unacceptable.

It is clear to me that there are undercurrent forces that seemingly work to short circuit a healthy relationship with her and the boys. I cannot exactly say where these forces originate, but it seems very apparent that they exist, and thus hinders effective interaction in the therapeutic sessions. Ms. attempts at all times to positively engage with the boys in session which is to her credit amidst resistance at times.

I took note that it was reported by the law-guardian Rebecca Smith that the boys have reported to her their unhappiness about

*the therapy sessions because "I ignore their concerns and seem
to be listening only to their mother." Ms. Rebecca Smith has not
called to express these concerns, but has seemingly accepted
their expressions with no regard for the truth.*

*Ms. Martinez has been putting forth a giant effort in the
therapy process to ensure that she can form a better relationship
with her sons against all that seems to oppose the same. Her
continued attendance in therapy to better herself and to connect
with her sons is proof of the same.*

*I submit this to indicate that Ms. Martinez makes a valiant
effort to connect with her boys and that her concerns for
unsupervised visits should be given consideration.*

Sincerely, Frank Johnson, Psy.D.

These notices consistently got ignored along with the police
reports I documented and Robert's previous criminal records I
submitted. What else is new? Rebecca Smith agreed to step down
as their legal guardian because I was surely challenging her
authority, but the judge denied my request for a new guardian for
the children. The story of my life- not being heard. This has been
taunting me from my childhood. All I am certain of is that my
God knows the truth and I'm satisfied with that. I refuse to break
down, reminding myself of how God has protected me in the past.
Even though this is painful, I know this is temporary.

The Decision and Order After Trial dated December 8,
2017, Robert was granted sole legal and physical custody of
our two children Jonathan- 7 years old and Louis- 9 years

old. I was to provide the child support and 50% of the mortgage payments made to the lender from the date of my breakdown November 3, 2015 to present, less any arrears Defendant owes on house payments, within sixty (60) days after service. Robert stopped making the house payments, almost leaving my home in foreclosure and he went back to court complaining he didn't receive enough money and the judge changed her decision and Robert was no longer held responsible for the arrears.

I was allowed supervised parenting time with an agreed upon supervisor, with alternating weekends from Friday, 6:00 p.m. until Sunday, 6:00 p.m. Once each work, I was entitled to unsupervised public place parenting time for three hours; and the parties shall alternate the holidays. I was granted supervised holiday and school recess. I was granted two non-consecutive weeks of supervised parenting time during the Summer each year with the children. The Plaintiff shall notify the Defendant each year in writing by April 15th as to which weeks I have selected.

The children and I were required to engage in therapeutic visitation. The parties shall endeavor to use an in-network therapist. However, if there is a cost associated with this Court Ordered therapy, the parties shall share the expense equally. I was ordered to continue with psychological and psychiatric therapy and treatment and shall comply fully with the treatment plan, including taking all medication as directed and provide proof of my attendance and compliance with treatment and medication on a monthly basis. Robert had to vacate the Marital Residence no later than ninety (90) days after the service of the Decision and Order After Trial. Robert was obligated to continue to pay all carrying charges, utilities and charges for the residence until he vacates including routine maintenance such as landscaping/snow removal.

I was responsible to remove the Defendant from the mortgage obligation within ninety (90) days after service of the Decision and Order After Trial. If the Plaintiff fails to remove the Defendant from said mortgage, the Marital Residence shall immediately be placed on the market for sale and the Defendant shall have the right to remain in the premises with the children until 48 hours prior to the closing on the sale of the house.

I was ready to sell my house because there was no way I would be able to get a loan to buy him out. I had no real income coming in since Wig Boutique was closed. Upon the sale of the house, I had enough equity to buy a co-op in the town of Babylon outright. I would only be responsible for the HOA fees. Instead, my parents paid off my house in cash and I found a tenant to help me pay my parents back with a legal promissory note.

Robert did not comply with the agreement. The lawn was not properly manicured. Weeds grew profusely and abundantly. He left me his unpaid utility bills and the mortgage payoff that were in arrears. If I did not receive a notice that my mortgage loan was being transferred to another company, I wouldn't have known about Robert's delinquency. When I called the new company, they informed me of the unpaid dues and how it will soon go into foreclosure if a payment plan is not scheduled. God is all knowing and protects me from trouble. I was so thankful for the timing of the mortgage transfer.

Robert was against the children going to family therapy because he knew the truth would emerge. I wanted to procure police reports documenting Robert's non-compliance with the agreement concerning the children's schedule with me. Of course, the male cops stick to the male's stories. They couldn't be bothered with my complaints. They shared, "Well how do we know that is the week you're supposed to have them? The divorce decree also doesn't state the exact days of the week that you agreed to." The officer implied that I was lying. I told him, "If that is the case then, how do other people make allegations without complete knowledge of the facts, in the case of harassment, rape or any other case for that matter." I then explained rationally, "Okay, I understand the point that you are making. Please tell me how I can correct this moving forward." My Divorce Decree had too many loopholes. I had to be persistent, persuasive and sound credible in my request. The officer seemed reluctant to help me. He finally typed up the report after I explained that I would need it for Family Court.

I received another letter in the mail notifying me that Robert was taking me to Appellate Court. He wasn't happy with the decision about the house and he did not want the children sleeping over at my parents' house. How can Robert possibly afford Trial and now Appellate Court? Meanwhile, I was still trying to pay off my credit cards. The lawyer representing Robert was a family friend. Yet again, I had to pay my attorney an additional $20K to write up my appeal. I probably didn't even need my attorney to represent me since Robert didn't have new substantial evidence to support his case. I was too scared to take my chances. Robert's case was denied.

After battling in court for five years, I learned not to be intimidated. While on the stand, I was trembling. I had to take deep breaths and ask them to repeat the question several times because legal jargon such as "objection, overruled" or "objection, sustained" would confuse me. I would try to figure out if I could answer the question or not. A few times I ended up answering the question when my lawyer refuted the response. I was so confused. I was never exposed to these courthouse phrases. Perhaps it's common sense to some of you, but I was oblivious. It's so intimidating when you answer the question and they re-word the same question again. Similar to a car accident deposition. You start questioning your response as if they didn't understand you the first time. The interesting thing is, you're not supposed to re-word your response. You need to keep reaffirming your response without giving into their manipulation. And quickly, I learned not to feel intimidated.

It was time for me to get over my fear of representing myself. Especially, because I had no choice. I had no more funds or credit card

> WHAT FEAR WOULD YOU LIKE TO OVERCOME?

allowances left to pay for representation. I went to the

courthouse and the clerk was helpful. She handed me the appropriate forms to fill out. I was so impressed with myself. I started to feel more confident and told myself that there were no consequences if I get this wrong. I'll just have to redo it until I get it right. I filed a Petition for custody. I filled out the appropriate forms so my parents could serve the documents to my ex-husband. I requested for the stars and the moon. Hoping for even a crumb, such as no supervision. Sadly enough, I got nothing. No star, moon or crumb. I may not have won custody over my children, but I gained character. What have you gained from a difficult situation?

My high school bestie Virginia told me, "There is no way you're selling your house to buy another house and still live in NY." It didn't make sense to her, but it made sense to me. I didn't want the memories associated with the house where we all once lived in. I wanted a new house to start a new chapter in my life. Virginia kept insisting, "Then sell your house and move away." I never imagined moving away all by myself without my boys. I have my successful store here in NY. Virginia stated that if she was with no kids and single, she would live her best life somewhere else. I knew she would, because she always does. She planted a seed. I thought, *but where would I go?* That's when I began contemplating my move. My son Louis was supportive of my decision to move away and told me to consider Texas. I asked, "Why Texas." He replied, "You don't have to wear masks and you can live comfortably." *I don't know anyone in Texas.* So, I considered Arizona because my favorite cousin Linda lives there.

Then Ryan reminded me that there are no beaches in Arizona. Oh yeah, it's a desert and beaches are important to me.

My sister Janice kept insisting I buy a home in Florida next to her as an investment. I then made a trip to Florida and started considering locations where I could open up another wig store. I rented an Audi convertible for a whole week scouting the Palm Beach area in Florida. I stayed at the Hilton Ft. Lauderdale Marina in a mini suite. I needed to feel, project, and manifest what the future looked like without settling for less. Those days of calculating every penny while married to make ends meet were behind me. Renting the Audi convertible reminded me of my single years before marriage, when I had my Volvo C70 convertible paid in full, traveling wherever and whenever I pleased. I was providing self-love back to myself once again.

I searched Pompano and Delray, Florida, to relocate my store. I called Sunshine Flea Market in West Palm Beach and they had a waiting list of forty other vendors awaiting a concession. I told the manager I had been running a wig business for over 20 years. She said, "I don't have a vendor who sells wigs so I will move you to the top of the list." Two weeks later, she called me and said, "We have an opening available." I immediately packed my wigs and mannequins in the trunk of my Lexus SUV and booked Amtrak. I moved in with my sister Raquel, until I could figure out my accommodation.

I searched Google for the most expensive places to live in Florida in 2021. Palm Beach was #1 so I started searching for places alongside the water so I could provide my parents access to my condo for them to enjoy. My mother always wished she had a house by the water. Every time my mother would go on a cruise, she would get a veranda with a water view. I started looking for condos along Flagler Drive with great views of the intracoastal waterway. The nearby bridge brings you onto the island of Palm Beach, Fl. My realtor Ron scheduled a few showings of properties that I had viewed online the same day. Ron was attentive as to where to park, punctual and suggested I see a high-rise property that had nothing available for purchase, but a rental available the next day. He explained, "Even if you have to wait till something becomes available, it will be well worth it. I just want you to see the amenities this building offers." In the meantime, I had to pretend I was interested in renting, not buying.

The next day, I was enamored with the superior building's fitness center, meeting rooms, entertainment facilities, catering kitchen, sauna, steam room, valet parking, clubhouse, hot tub, security and front desk attendant. The minute he took me to the rooftop pool lounge area I grabbed his arm and said, "This is it! This is what Virginia's cousin suggested I should buy. I don't need to look any further. I want to be in this building." I couldn't believe how God was connecting the dots for me and my future. I didn't even find it myself. This was God's vision for me through someone else's eyes because I couldn't even imagine this for myself.

Before I temporarily moved in with my younger sister Raquel, I took my kids to enjoy a surprise flight lesson at the Academy of Aviation in Long Island. I didn't want my ex-husband to sabotage this experience from me. I wanted my boys to think out of the box and build confidence that they can dream big and fly high. We flew over Jones Beach Theater and back to Farmingdale, NY, landing safely. Jonathan thought he was on an *Indiana Jones* adventure. Meanwhile Louis was petrified. I started to pray for traveling mercies before take-off. Louis stared at me strangely. I asked, "Are you embarrassed I'm praying out loud?" His reply was, "We're not going to die?" not realizing how terrified he was to launch. Once I told Louis it was his turn to fly, I explained how this would make an awesome Instagram post. He immediately forgot about his fear and hopped in the front and buckled himself in. Now that's my boy! What he wouldn't do for the ladies, am I right?

I wanted to make the rest of my time special. We then went to eat on the water in Bayville, NY and that experience wasn't as pleasant. I had to write their father an email which read, *Robert, I think it's really disgusting how you have those kids so scared of you. They couldn't even enjoy their meal because they were scared they would be late even after my dad called you to tell you we would be a bit late. Jonathan was starving until he saw the time and then didn't want to eat what he had ordered. He shared how he couldn't even enjoy it. And then I had to tell him that's very ungrateful. Try to reflect if this is really how you want to raise them with anxiety and not being able to enjoy their time with their mom. I also want to mention I will be away for 2 months and they're looking forward to seeing me and you're denying me a visit to a concert they so want to go to at Jones Beach Theater. I don't know who you think you're hurting. You're hurting them more than me. Reflect how your mom treated you and talked badly of your dad and you promised me you would never do that when we were married. And now here we are. Try not to repeat what you didn't like what was done to you as a child.*

When you become a believer of Jesus Christ, life doesn't automatically get easier. It just means the devil must work harder to entice you back to sin or make you doubt God. The devil is not threatened by you, when you're not a follower of Jesus. I just use my circumstance to build my character in Christ knowing the Victory is the Lords'. I'm never disappointed knowing Isaiah 64:8, "God is the potter and we are the clay. We are all the work of God's hands."

It says in the Bible Mark 10:29, when we hold our cross to follow Jesus and leave behind our loved ones, our blessings are multiplied by 100 times; with that comes persecution. This makes sense. When celebrities first become famous that's a blessing but when certain audiences become envious of other people's fame, they engage in gossip and the paparazzi cashes in because of the drama. The Lord is preparing me not to care about what anyone thinks of my story but God himself. I welcome your reviews on Amazon, good, bad or indifferent.

Life experiences have taught me to keep my emotions in check. Tell yourself feelings are not facts. I also tell myself hurting people hurt people. I prefer praying for my enemies for their healing so they don't have to hurt any longer, which God calls us to do. Just as Mathew 5:44 says, "Love your enemies and pray for those who persecute you."

CHAPTER FIFTEEN

CAN YOU USE SOCIAL MEDIA TO BE TRANSPARENT OR WOULD YOU CALL IT FAKEBOOK?

Posted on Facebook...*When you lose your children to your ex-husband and you still believe God can restore them back to you; I smile at the world knowing my father in heaven delivers on all his promises. I'm still in court fighting for my every other weekend with my children that was granted to me that my ex doesn't allow. I patiently wait for my victory and my promise from God. 4 years later, I'm still waiting and trusting. Don't give up whatever struggle you're enduring.*

Posted on Facebook...*What a heartfelt video. My son just shared that he felt excluded from one of his dear friends' birthday parties and I felt his pain. But God has made it clear to me that he does not set me aside but he sets me apart. I was lost for words of comfort. All I could say was, "It happens to all of us and I'm sorry you feel that way." I found this video the next day and all I could say is thank you Jesus that I could share this video with him and show him that God sets us apart from what's not good for us. Be thankful when we're excluded.*

Posted on Facebook...*Today I am emotionally drained. I went to Family Court and the system is a dragged out process. I felt unsuccessful. I'm just trying to enforce what was granted to me. It's been almost 3 long years. Sometimes it seems as though it will never end. But when you let go of the fight they are left fighting by themselves. So I've decided to let go and let God. I'm taking off my boxing gloves. Not sure myself what God has intended for my future but if his word promises he will fight my battles and I only need to stand still then I need to trust that in Exodus 14:14. 2 Corinthians 12:10, "For the sake of Christ, then, I am content with weaknesses, insults, hardships, persecutions, and calamities. For when I am weak, then I am strong. Keep building me up Lord because no one will steal my joy."*

I thank God for my trials and find it pure joy that he is building me up. I look forward to the day that God tells me, "Well done, good and faithful servant! You have been faithful with a few things; I will put you in charge of many things. Come and share your master's happiness!" Matthew 25:21.

Blog post...Welcome to our GRAND OPENING August 1st. We are excited to expand our wig store near Palm Beach, FL. It's time to spread our wings and step out in faith. God is opening up new doors to challenge my growth potential at the Sunshine Flea Market, West Palm Beach, Fl. Our New York Wig Boutique will continue to operate the same business schedule as usual.

Never in my wildest dreams did I ever imagine another wig store outside of New York. Thank you God for my best friend who saw a bigger vision for myself to inspire me to my fullest potential. She saw me so accomplished, and I just saw myself as just surviving. Now I want to truly believe it for myself by making her vision for me launch.

Our dreams can be intimidating but not impossible. Never allow fear to set you back from God's best. There is always something to learn from all the choices we make, whether good or indifferent. The only failure in life is not trying.

I expect this to be the most successful move I've ever made in my life. Leaving behind my two boys, close friends, my lovely parents and my successful Wig Boutique of over 20 years behind is probably the hardest decision I ever had to make. Now I have to start from scratch, rebuilding my new wig store venture and convincing my inner self that I can do this challenge. I have to remind myself that without sacrifice there is no gain.

As I work on my inward appearance of how I am accomplished, I want to help you with your outward appearance. Our fun, fabulous hairpieces, lovely wig collection including toppers and clip in extensions can make the whole difference. Every day I work on my appearance on the outside to match the inside. We look forward to meeting your friends and family members who reside or recently moved close to West Palm Beach, FL. Beauty is gained, inside as well as outside.

My Honda Pilot got worn out and retired at a junkyard. I then financed a Lexus. It was time to upgrade my life because I deserve it. Time to try new adventures and events. I did a Divas half-marathon 5K run and finished at 32:43 minutes. For my age, group 40-44, I came in 24th out of 268. I came in 167th out of 1,433 overall. Then I did a 5K bubble run. I jogged through ginormous cotton candy colored foam. And lastly, I did a 5K color run and left like a rainbow covered in colored cornstarch and baking soda. I just can't wait for my boys to continue the race with me in all aspects of life. They may enjoy the inflatable 5k run or a 5k mud run. I'm not fond of getting dirty, but in life you must run in the grind to finish at the top. I will run my race with grace even if mud encompasses me. Despite all my challenges, I was able to pay off my debt during COVID. I really can't explain how I was able to do that. All I know is I tithe faithfully and God provides the rest.

Since my divorce, I have used my JetBlue miles to travel around. I went to Arizona to visit my favorite cousin, Evelyn. We hiked Pinnacle Peak and Camelback Mountain. While I was there, she asked me if I knew Robert was bisexual. I asked "What do you mean?" She said, "You didn't see his Facebook profile page specifying he likes men and women?" I suppose I had seen his profile, but I didn't give it much thought. I like attractive men and women without being a lesbian, so I didn't think anything of it. It never crossed my mind he could possibly be bisexual. He always acted homophobic. Now it made sense why he never wanted to be intimate with me. Now I understand why he was telling everyone he didn't know how I got pregnant with Jonathan. Even today, I find it hard to believe he may be bisexual or gay.

One time, I gave my son a manicure and put clear polish on his nails and Robert flipped out and made Jonathan remove it immediately. Another time Louis wanted a baby doll and when I bought one for him. Robert made Louis get rid of it. I explained to Robert, "Louis only wants to copy you because you help me with changing Jonathan's diapers. Louis is only role playing as a father." Robert was using precautionary measures to ensure the doll does not become part of the toy collection in our home. Once we were divorced, the boys told me their dad took them for a manicure and pedicure and I guess his own rule went out the door. Robert was filled with double standards.

Robert's new girlfriend is a mother with a previous public criminal record driving under the influence with her infant son in the back seat of her car. She knocked on the front door of my house for the first time wanting to have a conversation with me. She introduced herself as Elizabeth and asked me if Robert was controlling. My response was, "He doesn't even let me see my boys! What do you think?" She shared a few stories of how he tries to intimidate her when she goes out with her girlfriends. I told her, "He is harmless." She said, he crosses his arms and does not leave the restaurant until she goes with him, making her uncomfortable. Looks like he found someone easier to control. She seemed submissive and was willing to tolerate his behavior. Perhaps she was better suited for him. She explained, she was in a marriage where her ex-husband was abusive. Now I understand how she could tolerate my ex-husband. She apparently lives around the block from me. I had never seen her in the neighborhood. How convenient, because Robert stalks my house each time before he visits her. I suppose he still is curious about my whereabouts.

I had the judges' written approval to take the children on a Disney Cruise with supervision. My ex-husband never provided their birth certificates so my children weren't able to board the ship. I lost the children's travel deposit and enjoyed the cruise with my older sister, Janice. I was devastated, but I refused to allow Satan to steal my joy.

I attended business events to keep up with the current fashion trends for Wig Boutique. I went to the ISSE Hair Show in California. I visited my friend who lived in Hollywood. As soon as I landed, my friend Miguel picked me up from the airport and drove me straight to Disneyland Theme Park. I then traveled to the IBS International Beauty Show in Las Vegas meant for members of the professional beauty industry. Afterwards I went ATV riding in the desert, visited the Skywalk of the Grand Canyon, hiked Red Rock Canyon and viewed the Hoover Dam.

Helena and I went to Atlantic City, NJ and stayed at several hotels. The Borgata Hotel Casino & Spa was a heaven to pamper yourself. The Ocean Casino Resort with a rooftop pool was unforgettable and Harrah's Resort waterfront shops were fun. I was swimming in the month of January on the rooftop with 80 degree weather. I'll never forget that day. I felt like I was living above the world and experiencing life as its finest under warm, cozy weather in winter.

I sailed on a K-love cruise to the Cayman Islands, and Cozumel, Mexico. Another bucket list excursion checked off. I went to a live Joel Osteen and Joyce Meyer event. Being single again afforded me the lifestyle I once had. I attended my first Christian concert Hillsong United at Madison Square Garden.

Lastly, I made it to Punta Cana, Paradisus, on December 1, 2018. I wanted to save the best for last. I attended a Pink-Tie Halloween Gala fundraiser for cancer, dressed as Wonder Woman. I figured if I'm celebrating an evil holiday I might as well have my armor of Christ on. I decided to be the newer version of Wonder Woman portrayed by Gal Gadot-Varsano to represent Ephesians 6:10-13, which says, "to put your full armor of God so you can stand against the devil's schemes. For our struggle is not against flesh and blood, but against the ruler's, against the authorities, against the powers of this dark world and against the spiritual forces of evil in the heavenly realism. Therefore, put on the full armor of God, so that when the day of evil comes, you may be able to stand your ground, and after you have done everything, to stand your ground, and after you have done everything, to stand."

I love the new version of me! I have finally learned to embrace myself with immense love and admiration. I was wearing my belt of truth. My breastplate of righteousness. My shield of faith. My helmet of salvation. My sword of the spirit is the word of God. My feet fitted with the readiness that comes from the gospel of peace (Ephesians 6:14-17). What superhero character are you?

The event was for a good cause and it was perfect for networking. Gina noticed me at the Pink Tie Gala while I was enjoying my own company dressed as Wonder Woman. She was dressed as the original Lynda Carter version of Wonder Woman. We made a connection and discovered she too wanted to escape life and make a quick getaway to Turks and Caicos. I made a deal with her- as long as we travel to Punta Cana Paradisus all inclusive, I'll go with her. In two weeks of just meeting each other, we were drinking pina coladas on the white sands of Paradisus. It was the long-awaited break I needed to rejuvenate myself.

I wasn't single for long; I met Anthony at a 4th of July party. I was so excited to finally meet a guy who seemed like he had it all together. He was 55 years old and retired from UPS. Don't be deceived by someone's profession. He made smart real estate investments and was a handy carpenter. He had several houses rented, worked overtime, and retired early. It felt too good to be true to meet someone who had it fairly together. Relationships always seemed to have a caveat. We went on several dates and I introduced him to a few of my girlfriends while we were out. He told my girlfriend's friend that he liked her shoes. I really don't think any guy should be complimenting anyone else besides the person he's with. Her stiletto heels were probably four inches high with a leather strap wrapped up her leg. We went out another night and we ran into a group of my acquaintances and again he proceeded to tell my girlfriends' sister he liked her high heel stiletto shoes with wrap around ankle straps. She replied, "I like Ava's shoes." Anthony's response was, "Ava's open-toe high heels are conservative." I felt secure for once because she was the only girl who redirected him correctly. I then explained to him, "In the future, if you like another woman's shoe, you tell me directly- Ava I like her shoes, those would look good on you." I told him, "If you want to see me again, you would have to buy me a pair of shoes." The next day he was at Bloomingdale's buying me a pair of high heels that were sparkly with embellished rhinestones. I couldn't believe he actually went to the store to redeem himself. I'm pretty confident of who I am, but his wandering lustful eyes were not going to work in this relationship. A month later, I eventually broke up with him on good terms. Anthony texted me a picture of this girl with short shorts, great legs and bright yellow high heels. I told Anthony, "Perhaps you should go up to her and ask her where she got her heels in case you were thinking of buying me another pair." We both laughed.

After this incident, I was done with men. I remained single for a whole year. A few days later, a new acquaintance named Daniele invited me to go to the Glen Cove Mansion for a networking event. Afterwards we went to a restaurant lounge. Daniele then introduced me to her friend Ryan who was divorced. He shared how he loved being married. Those words caught my attention because even though I didn't have a good marriage, I too loved being married. I asked him why he would say that? I didn't remember his response as he caught me off guard. He mentioned he has two boys and a daughter. I immediately told him, "I'm sorry, but I don't date guys with kids." His reply was, "That's okay. When they call, I'll just tell them there is no one here by that name." He made me laugh. I just wanted to get rid of him, so I told him, "I'm religious and I go to church. I don't think you would want to date a Bible girl." He said, "That's okay. I'll go with you this Sunday and I'll bring my son." I kept thinking, "Is this guy for real?" Ryan's humor and boldness captivated me to reconsider, what I never wanted to consider.

My criteria is a guy with no kids or an ex-wife. I wanted to close the gates for any type of drama. When Saturday approached, he told me, "I won't be able to go to church because my son Dillon doesn't want to go." I let him know, "This is why I don't date guys with kids. Children dictate their parents' life." I don't feel like being challenged by this type of conduct. Not even with my own kids. He immediately told me, "Wait, wait, give me another chance. I will get him to go next week." I was impressed that Ryan was so adamant to try to get this relationship off the ground. Sunday came and his son attended. Dillon kept his ear plugs on and stayed outside in the lobby area. Dillon refused to sit with us and listen to the sermon. I couldn't believe how disrespectful he was. I was just happy Ryan made the effort. I'm sure Dillon doesn't get away with disrespecting his mother. Ryan had this easy-going personality that anyone can take advantage of.

Ryan insisted on meeting my children. He wanted to attend their wrestling matches. I didn't think it would be a good idea because my ex-husband will make it harder for me to see my boys. Virginia had convinced me to gradually introduce Ryan as my friend. My children will eventually have to adapt to all these changing circumstances. I explained to my boys, "One day you will have a girlfriend and you will want me to be respectful towards her, so give your mom the same respect. Or would you prefer she dislikes me?" My children understood my logic.

For Easter, Ryan was going to meet my kids at my girlfriend's house for the first time. I figured a group setting should be better to ease my children into my new relationship. When Ryan arrived, Dillon refused to get out of the car and gave his dad a hard time. *Poor Ryan.* He arrived a bit late but didn't let Dillon dominate him. My sons even tried going to the car and asking Dillon to join them but he refused. On the weekends, when Ryan had Dillon, I tried to get him to warm up to me by playing charades using my phone app. At first Dillion didn't want to join in until he saw how much fun Ryan and I were having.

I had Ryan purchase a private booking for the *Escape Room* for Dillion to spend fun quality time with us. Dillon for the most part didn't want to get off his phone. Once Ryan threatened to disconnect his phone plan, Dillon shut off his phone an entered the escape room with us. It was my first time in a themed room on a mission to figure out riddles and clues to obtain the right keys or passcodes. It was fun trying to solve how to unlock the next room. I didn't even realize that my life was a combination of a series of events from which I wanted to escape.

Ryan's two older children weren't a piece of cake either. One was in college and the other one was in high school. The scams that Ryan's ex-wife devised to manipulate the kids to go against their father were disgusting. Ryan was temporarily laid off as an electrician from the Local 3 Union. His ex-wife, sister, and mother insisted that Ryan purchase his son's prom tuxedo. Meanwhile, his ex-wife collected more than a mortgage payment, and she was letting the house go into foreclosure and only responsible for utility payments. She collected her six figures as a teacher in tandem with alimony and child support from Ryan. His ex-wife still cried poverty. I didn't even receive that much from my husband while married and I still pay child support.

I told Ryan, "If you're going to buy his tuxedo, I think you should go with him to pick it out." Ryan asked his son, "What day do you want to go get your suit?" But his son insisted he wanted to go with his grandfather instead. Of course, because then his grandfather would pay for the suit and Ryan's son would pocket the money. On the day of prom, Ryan literally cried to me because his son posted pictures on Facebook with his prom date and Ryan was excluded. He was good enough for the money, but not good enough to attend the event. The scandalous behavior was so unwarranted.

The son and daughter only viewed him as an ATM machine. Once, I took Ryan's phone and texted his daughter the way Ryan should have handled her. "Victoria, I love you but would appreciate it if you didn't treat me like an ATM machine. I enjoy spending time with you but if you continue to treat me as an avoidant father then I will no longer fund you." Ryan got so mad at me. He said, "That's my daughter, I would never talk to her like that." I said, "Exactly, that's the problem, you don't know how to talk to her and set boundaries. You allow her to treat you how your ex-wife treats you; you are letting her be self-centered and entitled." I thought to myself, *who wants to get involved in a relationship with someone with all this drama going on?* That's why I didn't want to date someone who has children in the first place. I knew this would add conflict; I don't need more drama in my life.

One day, I couldn't take it anymore. Ryan's older brother started complaining about how Victoria was trying to scam her grandparents into cosigning her student loan. Meanwhile the grandparents are on a fixed income. Victoria promised her mother would make the payments. When Victoria's mother broke the agreement and stopped making the payments, Ryan's parents afraid that their credit would take a hit. They lived on a fixed income and now financial anxiety was haunting them. How will they be able to afford this unexpected payment?

During Mother's Day, Victoria didn't want to celebrate with her grandmother on a Saturday because she was busy. She asked if she could celebrate with Ryan's family on a Monday. Wow, this girl thinks Mother's Day revolves around her schedule. We should create a national holiday for entitled children and call it Teenagers Day. No appreciation for grandparents. I couldn't take it anymore. This began to affect me because Ryan doesn't deserve to be treated that way. Obviously, his ex-wife makes no effort to correct the behavior.

I sent Victoria an email letting her know, "I suggest you stop and apologize to your dad and grandparents for being disrespectful. Let your brother know presenting overinflated airline tickets to travel is manipulative as your dad was willing to pay. Most likely your mother used her frequent flyer miles instead. You were just trying to get over on your father. Both of you should be ashamed of yourselves. Both of you have no mercy. Your dad loves you so much he can't even confront you. I will not allow you to disrespect him. This cunning behavior will need to end. I'm all about you having a good relationship with your dad. When you learn to do what is right, I will respect you. Next time you see me say hello with manners. Not like what you did at the lacrosse game. Then we'll get along just fine. And I'll pretend we never had this conversation." Of course, Ryan was not happy that I confronted his daughter even though he knew I was looking out for his best interests. I told Ryan, "This is why I said don't date me. I have a voice and I will use it." I wanted my new relationships to be different from my marriage, where I couldn't speak. All I know is, what I texted worked because she didn't do it again. Since I got the results I had hoped for, I don't think I did anything wrong. She probably respects me more than Ryan and will think twice about how she treats her father.

I tried to break up with Ryan a few times before because I didn't see a future with us given all the drama. Same reason I didn't want to date Allen. I also didn't want to pursue a relationship that was unequally yoked, as stated in 2 Corinthians 6:14. To be yoked refers to two oxen that are joined by a wooden bar in order to complete work together. Being unequally yoked means that one ox is not equal in strength; one being weaker. Completing a task unequally yoked will be more challenging. My marriage felt like a seesaw, where I struggled trying to balance the weight of the relationship. I found myself trying to push forward while he was tugging me back.

Ryan came to church with me, but I knew he was there for the wrong reasons. I needed God's truth to be my standard, otherwise I knew I would be engaging in more self-harm. Life isn't an easy task to live up to God's standard. We are in constant battle with the lies we believe causing us to compromise God's truth. Another reason I knew that Ryan and I wouldn't work out is because he would want to randomly look through my phone. That was the perfect opportunity for me to look through his phone. Not sure what Ryan was looking for. He really didn't find anything to feel insecure about. I would go to Ryan's deleted photos and I found pictures of girls that were almost his daughter's age. He probably downloaded it from a dating site or Instagram. I just know men are usually never happy with what is in front of them. I also saw notifications from the Tinder dating app on his phone once. We would break up but he would still show up at my house after midnight a bit drunk. I would let him sleep it off. He always woke up in a good mood and made me crack up again, forgetting why he upset me in the first place.

One day, Ryan thought it would be funny to play creepy music in my apartment because he knew I was such a fanatic. He didn't realize I would freak out and run under the covers and start to cry. He immediately shut off the eerie music and came under the covers and started to cry with me. I told him, "Don't cry with me. You are making it worse." He felt so bad he did that to me. He didn't expect me to be so terrified. The satanic music made me fearful of suffering from bipolar disorder again. I didn't want Ryan bringing demons into my apartment like my ex-husband did. Ryan doesn't understand spiritual warfare. However, Ryan does have dreams where he subconsciously battles his demons. When he would stay over at my house, he would make frightened noises in his sleep. I would slightly nudge him so he wouldn't feel tormented. Occasionally Ryan slept over because his commute to work was closer. Before we would go to sleep, I would pray so he wouldn't have bad dreams.

Ryan and I eventually broke up. I had my friend Jimmy come over a few weeks later and help me install a 3D mural wallpaper in the basement. I made dinner for us afterwards and Ryan comes storming into the house with the spare keys saying, "Hi, I'm Ryan I was here yesterday. I'm here to get my belongings and condoms." Ryan was definitely drunk. He immediately went to the basement but my mattress was no longer there. I moved the mattress upstairs days ago. I had been remodeling the house. Obviously, Ryan was just trying to make Jimmy believe we were still in a relationship. Ryan asked, "So tell me, what work did she have you do in her house?" Jimmy disregarded the question and gave Ryan a handshake while wishing him a goodnight like a gentleman and took his tools. That was the perfect time for Jimmy to exit because I don't like drama. I made sure Ryan left my house as well.

There isn't one person I don't tell that I will remain celibate till marriage. My own friends didn't believe me and one time they asked Ryan, "Tell us the truth, Ryan. You still don't have sex with Ava?" He replied, "I tried today and the answer was still no." I was so proud that he wasn't embarrassed to tell the truth. Our relationship lasted two years so everyone found it hard to believe. Our connection was still affectionate and our communication was hardly ever misunderstood, which impressed me. I remember when I used to talk to my ex-husband and share my feelings, I wouldn't get any response back. I felt ignored most of the time. Whereas, Ryan would try to come up with a solution, which really made me feel heard. The complete opposite of what I had.

I am well aware of the scripture, Thessalonians 5:22 to avoid any behavior anyone might perceive as inappropriate. I definitely was compromising my faith by having Ryan sleepover. This is a behavior I wouldn't want my children to emulate. Sure, it is easier to push your standards down rather than drag it upwards. Dating someone with the same standards that God requires is important to me moving forward.

Ryan and I remained friends until I packed up my stuff and moved to Florida. He found himself a girlfriend exactly the way he liked. She had beautiful long dark hair, with exaggerated boob implants and a tattoo sleeve on her muscular arms. Yet he continued to call me, saying how he felt like he was cheating on me. I then realized he slept with her and I asked him to never call me again. I would never want to date a guy who maintains a relationship with his ex-girlfriend. I don't want it done to me so I wouldn't want to do that to her. Leaving my children and Ryan to create a better life for myself was the second hardest thing I ever had to do besides divorce.

CHAPTER SIXTEEN

MY DEAR GOD LETTERS AND WHY WE SHOULDN'T REPEL OUR FRENEMIES.

August 3, 2021, *Lord, I'm off to start a new chapter in my life. I'm closing on a condo in downtown Florida with a large heated rooftop pool. This was exactly what Virginia's cousin suggested I should get. A beautiful high rise overlooking the intracoastal with a rooftop lounge. I couldn't even imagine this for myself. I feel like I'm going through a second divorce leaving behind my children, New York and Ryan. I thought leaving the relationship we had would be easier. Thinking back, I remember Robert and I were both asked to separate for thirty days by two different pastors. I know that was confirmation from God to separate. Robert found it difficult to follow the rules. This time Lord, you have completely removed me from Ryan and all I do is listen to the lyrics of music to try to find comfort in what you want to tell me. Songs I've never heard of before are really relating to my soul.*

Ryan had such a cheerful gentle spirit about him, unless he got jealous. My children loved Ryan which attracted me more to him. His family values were similar to mine. Lord, where am I going? This is the first time in a long time my heart is broken. I can't even picture dating anyone else. Even if I tried to start a new relationship, deep down inside I would still be saddened. I remind myself that Ryan couldn't care for me the way I wanted him to. But if I was wrong Lord, reveal it to me one day. As I will wait. Heal my heart precious Jesus. I am less sad Lord knowing you are in control. Otherwise, Lord, perhaps I will wait for your very best. I'm open to whoever that person may be. I just need to be still and obedient. No man is coming into my life benefiting from what I have until I know they're all invested with me first. My ex-husband took everything from me and I'll be damned if someone tries to take advantage of me again.

August 6, 2021, Thank you Lord for speaking to me today through this scripture, Luke 9:57-62. I truly want to dig deeper into your word. Let's break it down verse by verse. Verse 57 says, "I will follow you where you go." And Jesus said to him, "The foxes have holes, and the birds of the air have nests, but the son of man has nowhere to lay his head." Wow that was mind blowing to me. I don't know where I'm laying my head at night. I'm unsettled in my life, displaced from my home, removed from my children. I understood the scripture meant that when we follow Jesus, it won't be a comfortable or an easy path. I have no foresight as to what the plan is, where I'm going to end up and why. This seems trivial to me but I guess it is a major part of your plan. The verse 58 continues to read, "And he said to another, "follow me." But he said, "permit me first to go and bury my father." But he said to him, "Allow the dead to bury their own dead." It sounds reasonable to want to bury your father first before you leave to follow Jesus. But from Jesus' standpoint, we usually tell Jesus, "How about later or another day when it's more convenient." I try to put Jesus first in my life. I like to start my mornings in prayer and end my nights with praise and worship. But there are days I make excuses. I gave this more thought. Instead of saying Lord, let me tend to my dead father first. We should ask the Lord, "how can we make sure my dad is buried properly before we go?" For me I would like to believe most people don't know how to communicate properly. It makes a world of difference when we rephrase the same concern. The next person in the scripture wants to say goodbye to his family before he leaves, which is also reasonable to ask. So that's why this parable seemed difficult to see from Jesus' perspective. The problem with that wish to say goodbye was that he was making excuses not to follow or was simply procrastinating. He wanted to keep his options open and stay where he was more interested. This reminds me of Ryan with his excuses and a lack of desire to follow Jesus after witnessing several miracles in his personal life and his interest in looking at more attractive women to reclaim his youth. Oh Lord, forgive me for the excuses I made for staying in that relationship longer than I should have. As much as I tried to get away, my flesh was so weak.

But Lord, I now understand we can't do things in our own flesh. I couldn't control that weakness persisting within me. Quickly, I discovered I had to dig into the Holy Spirit to give me the strength. I want to Thank you Lord for pulling me away. Now I'm in another state and I am ready to follow you without unhealthy distractions. I had to block Ryan, otherwise my emotions would get the best of me. He moved onto someone else quickly. Therefore, I refuse to remain friends with him while he is with another woman. As I wouldn't want that done to me. So, I'm giving Ryan a clean handshake goodbye so he can really have what he desires, which wasn't me. He didn't know how to be all in. Lord, I'm all in again with you. You are the only person who protects me, spoils me, loves me with all my imperfections. You know me better than I know myself. I sit here at Sunshine Flea Market with little sales but I am comforted to be away from all the drama of my ex-husband, my parent's supervising my visitations as court ordered, my children not standing up for me and Ryan not truly committing. I feel free. This isn't easy Lord, following your path, but I trust you. I may feel free but my heart still needs mending.

August 7, 2021 I'm still crying Lord, I wish I can tell Ryan I'm sorry I pushed him away. I programmed his head that we were just friends. I spelled it out to him so many times. I loved his persistence and confidence. That was so sexy. He knew he could fix anything. His communication to resolve our conflicts was impeccable. Ryan asked me to post pictures of us on social media. As well as add to my profile status that I'm in a relationship. He also wanted me to meet with his children over dinner and discuss our differences so we could get along better. He truly suggested many things to make our relationship work but Lord I was too scared to get serious. I give so much credit to Ryan for trying. Ryan had a magnifying happiness. Not too many things would rock his world, except his ex-wife. It bothered me when his ex-wife still had his emotions entangled. But Lord Ryan did so well in court when she was seeking more money. Ryan started demonstrating more self-control over his emotions when addressed by the judge. I'll never forget he told me, "Ava I was married for twenty years, so give me some time and I will undo what I was previously conditioned to." What he shared was a fair assessment. I don't even know what real love looks like except for the sacrifices I have made in my past relationships. And I probably convinced myself that Ryan wouldn't make the same sacrifices for me. I was scared to invest in someone who doesn't invest in me first. Especially when I have so much too lose. I'm tired of men benefitting from me and only getting crumbs from the relationship.

So many times, I wanted to send a song I heard on the radio to Ryan that reminded me of us. I just heard a song and I laughed because we would always banter with music.

Ryan wasn't coming to visit me in Florida and that's when I discovered there was someone else. I had anticipated this but didn't realize how this would hurt in the long run. Lord, help me forgive myself for pushing him away and help me to forgive him for hurting me this way. He doesn't even know how I bleed over this. But I convinced myself that I'm making this sacrifice for him because I felt he didn't love me enough. Lord, if I'm wrong for what I did you will reveal it to me. But I never want to be in a tangled web with another woman. I remember my friend Maria's story. The other woman wouldn't go away, even if she did try to reconcile her relationship. So, Lord, I will just leave. I hope Ryan is happy now. Just like the song I just heard. Meanwhile, I'm suffering probably more than him. Lord, I trust you will honor my obedience. I know you will fill my heart one day. Help me not to keep obsessing over Ryan. Help me to keep praying for your fullest potential in my life. I pray for Ryan's happiness with you in it, Lord. Give Ryan the courage to stand on stage one day with his amazing talent of humor and wit because he makes so many people laugh naturally. I believe in him so much. I pray one day he can believe it for himself.

Today, I discovered I need someone with the same goals to be aligned with me. I texted my friend Rick in Boca and asked, "Why are nice guys weak?" His response was, "They play it safe and don't take risks." Risk-takers demonstrate faith, determination, and are not scared of failure. Rick wrote back, "you are better off with a risk taker. It's your personality. My dad plays it safe and his wife is the same. They are very happy and live a nice life. Everyone is different." I realized the key is to find someone who is similar to me. Maybe that's why I'm frustrated. I don't attract risk takers. I feel like a unicorn.

Well Lord, I'm just going to wait to see what you unveil to me. We're all your children and you want us all to be happy. Thank you, Lord, for all the sermons I'm listening to help me heal and learn to forgive Ryan so I don't hurt anymore. I unblocked Ryan today because I don't want to put walls between us. I did it so I can heal. Plus, I don't agree with him playing with my emotions while he's with someone else. I hope he is uncomfortable without me. Or maybe grow to love her in a healthy way without distractions. Perhaps I should have been more honest with him at the beginning. I thought I was and felt ignored. Allow me to forgive him the same way Ryan forgave me in the past. Give me your strength today. All I know, Lord, is you have something amazing for all of us.

I must learn to take one day at a time and enjoy the moment. Genesis 19:36 says, "But Lot's wife looked back, and she became a pillar of salt." I don't want to be stuck in time looking at the past. Yesterday I enjoyed my jog after work. Today I enjoyed my two sales and my quiet time listening to Christian sermons. I enjoy my music and most of all, I enjoy you Lord, giving me instructions and allowing me this time to dig deeper into your word.

I read Mark 9:23-29, "If you can?" Said Jesus, "Everything is possible for him who believes." Immediately the boy's father exclaimed, "I do believe; help me overcome my unbelief!" ...Then the disciples asked Jesus privately, "Why couldn't we drive it out?" Jesus replied, "This kind can come out only by prayer." Ryan never said he's an unbeliever. Ryan said he has his doubts. Doesn't make him an unbeliever. Ryan does believe but needs help with his unbelief. I want to pray that you, Lord, remove the deaf and mute spirit in him. Do I still believe God can do the impossible? Perhaps, sometimes I have unbelief also. Was I for Ryan? Is Ryan for someone else? Would he be able to live in Florida and start from scratch with me? Would he be able to do long distance together without him surfing the internet? I too have so many doubts. Is he capable of loving me? Will I feel safe or number one alongside Jesus? So, I pushed him away because of my own doubts. Show me Lord if I was wrong. I don't doubt the fact that I'm supposed to be in Florida. Even if business is a bit slow, I know in my heart I am right where you want me. I'm comforted by that fact. But help me overcome my other disbeliefs.

I sometimes doubt if there is someone for me, meanwhile everyone else has someone to help them heal while I heal alone. This is the worst feeling. Relationships are not easy. Thinking back to my past, when I walked away from Rick in Connecticut before I got married, I remember how I would rollerblade down the bike path to Jones beach. Then I got divorced and I found myself on the bike path telling myself, here I am again on the same path trying to heal from Ryan. The hardest break-up and now jogging a new path in Florida for healing. I blocked Ryan because I called late one night and he couldn't pick up and I realized he's out with someone else and again, I came second. Why am I calling? When will I come first in someone's life? I'm constantly on my knees.

Ryan doesn't know how to be alone. Most men move on so quickly without healing and working on their emotions. This is my time to heal and love myself first. Help me Lord, show me what's really going on with my children. Show me what's really lurking behind my disbelief. Help me overcome it. Someone posted on Facebook, "If you want to fly, you have to give up the things that weigh you down." I don't hate Ryan. I just wish he loved me more. When will someone see my value? I've been running the path far too long. I want to stop running alone.

Give me your peace today. Allow me to enjoy each day. I need to live in the moment. These raw emotions are getting the best of me. Thank you, Lord, for where you have me. Everyone here in Florida thinks I'm Brazilian. Perhaps because of my Spanish accent. I can't wait to make new friends in my new condo.

August 8, 2021, Today I rid myself of my disbelief. I will tell myself, "I will never be alone." "God will never leave me nor forsake me" says Deuteronomy 31:8. I walk with Jesus and Jesus walks alongside me every path I take. Every time the thought that I'm alone creeps up in my head, I will remember that's a lie. I know my worth and only the right person deserves me. I will not settle for crumbs and it is unfortunate for the people I leave behind not to recognize it. That's all I can tell myself until it really penetrates deeper and deeper in my spirit.

I've unblocked myself so Ryan can get in touch with me, Lord. If I'm still on his mind he will contact me. Doubt creeps in and then I tell myself he may not. Lord, I'm going to be positive and hold onto the songs that comfort my heart, "I'm halfway gone." Pain is good. Discomfort is good. I'm a warrior. I can handle this. No pain, no gain. Regardless, Lord, I will pray for Ryan to one day be freed from the lies of his unbelief.

Okay Lord, I apologized to Ryan for not giving him a fair opportunity. He too did so many things for me not to trust him. Lord, I'm preparing my heart to be ready, in case he chooses her over me. I will be okay. He admitted he can be vindictive. When I was protecting him against his daughter, he was threatening to call the law guardian. He acted like my ex-husband trying to hurt me. One time Ryan splashed water on me just for saying hi to a guy friend but he was allowed to flirt with my friend Robin and Clarissa. Lord, you are thickening my skin. I need to upgrade my relationships with men and make sure they're an asset not a liability in my life. My great life is in front of me, not behind me. The past was just for the lessons.

August 10, 2021, Good morning, Lord, today I love myself, I accept the pain of my past because it has gotten me to the place where I am now. It's a bit scary but exciting. Scary because a beautiful condo is just a building. I can still feel empty inside but Lord that's the work in progress you are going to restore in me. I am going to forgive the pain because I'm getting stronger.

I thank Ryan for pushing me towards moving to Florida. He reminded me that Arizona has no beaches and then I considered Florida. He mentioned his mom used to travel back and forth on Amtrak when she lived in Florida. Lord, Ryan encouraged me to relocate and I thank him for that. I thank my ex-sister-in-law for meddling in my marriage because I have a new marriage in Christ. The Lord is going to elevate me in such a way I won't even believe it's true. I still feel as if this is all surreal.

I thanked my oldest sister Silvia for putting down my dreams of being an art teacher or interior decorator. I sometimes regret throwing out my art portfolio because she told me there was no money in art. My art teacher told me I could probably get a scholarship for my talent. But Silvia's opinion mattered more to me. I knew I had my parents' approval so I was more concerned about what my older sister thought because I looked up to her. Silvia's insults made me work harder to prove I will be somebody big one day. That is why I opened my own business and I bought my first home by myself at twenty-nine years old. I probably wouldn't be so ambitious if I didn't have to prove it to myself and her. I thanked her for making me feel like I had a big nose, which I used to mush against the wall to try to flatten it because my appearance makes me humble. I prefer people telling me I'm pretty and trying to make myself believe it, rather than be conceited.

Two and a half years later, Anthony was trying to get in touch with me but I had him blocked. I had 32 missed messages from

Anthony which I didn't even realize. He was trying to invite me to travel to Aruba with him. He has had this beautiful girlfriend for the past two years and he's still trying to call me. He tattooed Proverbs 8:35 on his chest a year ago, "For whoever finds me finds life." He knew scripture would impress me. His eyes wandered toward younger women. He's struggling with age. As much as he wants to settle down with one person, he still desires much younger women without children so it does not conflict with his lifestyle. What he desires is different from what his eyes tell him. He's dating an attractive, muscular lady of his age and he still isn't happy. The only person who can fill Anthony's void is Jesus.

Ryan tried calling me on multiple occasions while he was dating someone else because I was moving to Florida. As painful as it was to leave Ryan, he deserves someone else. Everyone in my family loved Ryan including my children. I want to be happy for his new relationship. Ryan was more discreet with the eyes so the relationship lasted longer. But there were occasions when Ryan was discreetly checking out the other moms at my son's PTA meetings. The only reason I knew this was because I told him, I myself was checking out the women and felt most of them were letting themselves go. Ryan agreed by responding he too had a difficult time selecting someone pretty. I was definitely fishing for a different response from him such as, "Ava you were the prettiest in the room. I'm glad we're together." Anthony and Ryan are no different. Both looked at the superficial aspects of people instead of the interior and still called me because they were attracted to Jesus residing within me. But they were too scared to give up their lustful ways. I need a spirit filled man with a whole lot of purpose. I know I will never be enough for anyone who doesn't have God centered in his core.

So, I choose myself to be happy with and date myself every day. It requires a strong mindset and positive reinforcement of self-talk. I'm married to Jesus. Don't worry, I promise never to elope again. I would only entertain a relationship if we sharpen each other (Proverbs 27:17) for God's purpose. I would hate to miss out on God's promise by compromising my faith. Moses was banned from the Promised Land because of one little incident of disobedience striking the rock instead of speaking to it as instructed in Numbers 20:8-12. Failure to trust the Lord's holiness blocked his own blessing.

I posted on Facebook, "Everyday has been challenging for me. Leaving my children and loved ones behind in New York and starting over has not been easy. When I arrived in Florida, my car was vandalized. My rear passenger windows shattered as soon as I shut the front door. I had to use a temporary garbage bag around the car door until I could get it fixed. Luckily, my car insurance covered the expense. The same day I got news that my mortgage loan may not get approved and I may lose my $15k deposit on my high-rise condo in West Palm Beach. The 5% down payment will not be enough and they require 15% down on the property in addition to my Lexus 350 paid in full. Not sure if I will have the funds to make this happen by November 4th. Unlike in New York, in Florida, the realtor writes up the contract, not real estate lawyers. My contract states the approval must be within 30 days. The bad news was given to me outside of the 30 days. My closing date is three months out because there is a tenant occupying the space. Well Lord, I stand on scripture verse Psalms 62, "I WILL NOT BE SHAKEN." I love peanut butter and jelly, I will survive this. The enemy is just making my story juicier for you readers to learn how I overcome the storms. My life is an adventure and quite a journey. What I have overcome makes me more fearless in Christ. I meditate on Psalms 62, "O my soul, in God alone; my hope comes from him. He alone is my rock and my salvation; he is my fortress," I WILL NOT BE SHAKEN. My circumstances may be out of my control but I'm safe knowing God is in control."

My Christian friend from New York responded to my Facebook post, *Ugh Ava. I am so sorry! Maybe it is time to come home… maybe the Lord might be showing you something different than you think? Anyway, regardless of the decision…we are praying for you in the life group.* I thought to myself, *why is she feeling sorry for me? I know my victory is coming.* I then realized the truth behind *misery loves company.* Sharing anything positive to someone who isn't positive is upsetting to them. She is suggesting how she would just give up and act defeated. *Why would I join her?* I replied, *Sorry, I know my outcome will be amazing. I'm not coming to New York. The enemy is just trying to shake me and he can't.* These are the reasons why I'm a social Introvert. I don't need people to inflict their doubt onto me. After jumping through hoops to get this condo, I think I will join the circus and partake in all the stunts to get to where God is taking me.

Helena from New York was inquiring how I was doing in Florida. I shared with her via text, *I struggle everyday with my emotions, but I put them back in check with God's promises.* Helena texted me she saw Ryan and then left me curious to ask more as bait to hurt me. I texted back, *thanks for sharing about Ryan, but it still hurts so I think I would rather not know in the future.* Her response was, *I agree, that is the reason I was trying to avoid your questions. You looked amazing on Facebook. I am impressed with your dancing skills.* Insult with flattery got me fueled because I was trying to be civil about her deceitful actions. I don't know what question she was referring to because I never inquired further. I replied via text, *Yes, but just by saying you saw him, you made me curious. And then you left me hanging; wasn't cool. Either you tell me the whole thing or don't tell me at all. If you think it may hurt me, then don't tell me. Did you do that on purpose? By saying you were avoiding the question makes you guilty trying to bait me and then trying to deflect the story onto me as if you're innocent. That's very manipulative.* Her response was, *What is your problem? You should know me better than that! I am not entertaining this conversation. I told you about Frank and Anthony as well. You only asked about Ryan! I avoided telling you he was with his girlfriend because I took you into consideration and put myself in your position. It hurts as it did for me with Tom, if you remember! I didn't appreciate your comments toward me as a person.* I let her know, *I've known you to be manipulative on other occasions. You did it when you were late to my house because you wanted me to drive. You were causing me anxiety by being late and excusing your actions by telling me how my parents help me and you have no one to help you so that should excuse you from being late on a regular basis.*

You also added how I should understand that you were arguing with Tom, which led you to be late. You didn't make sense twisting and intermingling stories, meanwhile you were late on three other occasions. A simple sincere apology would have been sufficient. I'm being a friend right now by being honest about your unwarranted repetitive actions. You tried to take advantage of me another time. I was okay with driving 3 hours to Atlantic City. You also wanted me to pick you up, front door service because you couldn't inconvenience your son to drop you off. Not sure why you couldn't leave your car at my house. But it was okay to inconvenience me an extra hour out of my way. Knowing I had to go straight to work when we returned. It's okay Helena. That is why I'm a social Introvert because people like to hurt people. No hard feelings. I'm not angry. Just pointing out the obvious and if that bothers you then I'm sorry. But we can't grow if people don't point things out to each other. Her response was, *Deal with your own demons. Obviously, you don't seem to know me! Remember I was the first person and the only one that took you into consideration. I am nothing but honest and always spoke the truth that maybe you don't like. As you said, sorry if the truth hurts! You should go pray because you are being manipulated by the enemy? I am not giving him ammunition because he is using you to affect me. I rebuke in the name of Jesus!!! I could point many fingers at you and tell you many things, but I am not playing your game. Including you having a birthday party for people that you just met and not me.*

I thought to myself, famous rebuking terms Christians who are not well versed in scripture like to use. We are not to rebuke others, only God judges. People are always expectant and that is why I'm a social Introvert. I suppose she forgot that we went to Carlton on the Park on her birthday and I was able to get us in the private Clubroom for members only by requesting the host to please seat us as I'm trying to do something special for my friend's birthday. I ignored her last text response and let her have the last word. I no longer need to defend myself. I know my own truth and I can now be at peace and satisfied with it. I've come a long way.

I had sent an email to another frenemy that same week. Boy, was I emotionally exhausted. The email read, *I just want to share that I'm taking a break from everyone in New York. I'm going through a lot of pain with Helena who is trying to poke at my already existing love wound. I was told I could lose my $15K deposit if I don't come up with an additional 10% down payment and pay off my car by November 4th. Also, my sister Janice's mentally abusive ex-boyfriend put some chemicals in her shampoo and her hair got all tangled. Janice called me in the middle of the night hysterically crying because she thought she would have to shave her whole head. Right before I came to Florida, I had an allergic reaction to the keratin treatment and my face swelled like a pumpkin. I couldn't even open my eyelids. I feel my sister's pain. I know I expressed my pain clearly, but you didn't seem to want to hear what I said. You wanted to hear something else because you clearly said, "Ava why don't you just tell the truth, you wish you were married, you wish you had your kids, you wish your business would take off." We already knew all that, so why did you have to remind me of an already pre-*

existing injury? I learned that people who don't like to listen only want to hear what they want to hear."

Even when I told you I'm not having sex till marriage you tried to tell me to contradict God's word, otherwise I wouldn't find anyone. You had to ask your contractor Rick if he would date a girl who isn't having sex till marriage. He confirmed that a guy looking for a good woman would appreciate that. Just because you're doubtful doesn't mean I have to be. I accept whatever God has in store for me.

I did a live streaming interview for my upcoming book and my heart felt heavy to divulge my personal life. Most likely I sounded unprepared and misunderstood. All you focused on was, "Why did the interviewer say you have a good relationship with your kids when you don't?" I have known you for a long time to not take things personally. I know my relationship with my children, so I didn't allow your words to hurt me. My relationship with Louis and Jonathan may not be perfect but it's great considering the circumstances. It was refreshing that the interviewer, who hardly knew me, shared that I'm still close with my children. I only want to surround myself with people with positive vibes. *When you're ready to be a real friend I welcome you back. For now, respect my space until I'm in a better place. I don't have room for more accidental injury.*

I then sent an additional email saying, *I would like to remind you that when I was sharing with you, I didn't know which condo to get, you attacked me and said, "Why are you trying to copy my life?" This didn't even make sense to me. I calmly told you, "How can I copy your life? Even if I wanted to copy your life, I couldn't*

because God's in control. Not me! I'm still single and I already own a property in New York so I don't need to copy your life."
That is when you made me aware you were my frenemy.

Of course, I know it wasn't an accidental injury, but I decided to offer the same grace God gave me. I'm assuming they didn't do it on purpose but I'm aware of their actions. "Forgive them for they do not know" as Jesus said it best at the cross in Luke 23:34. I didn't realize until that day how tolerant I could be against hurtful behavior when I remind myself of scripture verses. People don't know their limitations. My fault for allowing myself to be mistreated for so many years. I am accountable for letting them be hurtful towards me by not communicating what offends me. I find even more grace when I hold myself equally responsible for my actions. I am so proud of myself because I was initially going to ignore her behavior without addressing it. But God revealed to me, Proverbs 28:23, "In the end, people appreciate honest criticism far more than flattery." Virginia was that girlfriend who made me feel like she was my cheerleader. She made me feel admired and lifted my ego when I felt small. But God has revealed to me in Romans 16:18-19, "By smooth talk and flattery they deceive the mind of naive people. Everyone has heard about your obedience, so I am full of joy over you; but I want you to be wise about what is good, and innocent about what is evil." Thank you, Lord, for such a revelation so I can be a better friend with truth and love and just hope they learn to understand the way you, father, have taught me.

During Covid, Virginia shared with me that she was jealous of me because I sent her a video of me and Ryan exercising to

Zumba on YouTube in his small one-bedroom apartment. Music excites my spirit. How could she be jealous of that? She can do Zumba in her new luxury home by the water. She moved there during Covid. The backyard looks like a resort. Her master bedroom on the second floor has this charming balcony and a Jacuzzi and sauna in the restroom. Virginia continued to tell me how she is jealous of me because I have met celebrities, I travel the world, and how I'm so successful with my business. The way she described me was so flattering. It didn't even sound like me.

I actually wanted to meet the person she was describing. I never saw myself as successful because I always felt like I was financially struggling to make ends meet. I always had nice things but I hustled to have them and to give my children a better life. I asked her, "What celebrity did I meet?" She told me I met a social media influencer with alopecia. I remember telling her when I went to Vegas to attend a Hair Solutions Conference and I was shocked to meet the model in my wig catalog. She approached me as if I was famous. She greeted me and said, "You are the owner of Wig Boutique?" I thought to myself, *She knows me?* She was excited to share the fact that she bought her first good quality wig from me when she was 14 years old. I didn't recognize her because she was so grown up. She is also a social media influencer who always dreamed of being a model. She thought the hair loss would interrupt her dreams. But instead, it made her more beautiful and got her noticed. Her dream became her reality. She now embraces her new, yet diverse appearances with assurance and gratitude with or without a wig. She has her very own YouTube channel and is leaving her footprint to inspire other women. I felt such gratitude to be remembered as I always felt like I go unnoticed because I was a social Introvert.

I never knew where I fit in socially. In high school, I tried out for cheerleading and basketball and didn't make the cuts. So, I focused on working hard at McDonalds when I was 14 years old. I was promoted to Crew Chief. Then I went to work for a law firm as a Spanish translator and legal secretary in my senior year of high school. I used to go to school in business casual attire and carried a leather attaché bag instead of a backpack to school. Wow, I never realized how unusual I was until I began to reminisce. No wonder I didn't fit in. I was different for sure.

I shared with Virginia that I appreciate the flattery or jealousy as I accepted it from a sincere heart. Later on, I learned in Jeremiah 17:9, "the heart is more deceitful than all else and is desperately sick, who can understand it?" I sure can't. I asked Virginia, "How can you admire my life? I may dance often, but I'm struggling mentally, juggling my finances, and I don't have a lifelong partner like you do to help me." I always wanted to be an amazing housewife and have a recreational job or volunteer somewhere. It amazes me how people believe value comes from work or accomplishments. Good works doesn't get you into heaven either. Ephesians 2:8-9 say, "For it is by grace you have been saved, through faith; and this is not from yourselves: it is the gift of God: not by works, so that no one can boast."

Virginia owns a four-story brownstone in Washington Heights, Manhattan, also known as Spanish Harlem from her divorce. She also owns a house on the water exclusively on her name because of her current husband. I told her, "I admire your life because everything you have comes from God freely." I would never be ashamed if I got things freely from God. The misconception here is that many people believe we have to earn our value. God has given it to us for freely. I suppose many people have a hard time believing that. Value comes from Galatians 5:4, "The only thing that counts is faith expressing itself through love." I believe what she truly admires is my faith. I don't have much to envy after my divorce. I just have my Heavenly Father, *Mr. Big* shielding. I was living in the attic of my house, renting the downstairs to make ends meet. I came home to an empty house every night. I used to come home as late as I could, so I didn't have to be reminded I'm alone. After several months, I accepted my new life. *Time to enjoy my new space.*

To me, jealousy means you're saying to yourself, *you can never have that.* I was never jealous of my girlfriend even though she would brag about how fabulous her husband treats her. How he sends her romantic text messages each day and the flowers never stop coming. I just kept reminding myself that I, too, will have that one day. That's how I was able to rejoice in her happiness. But one day I had to tell her, "I'm crying right now and I'm sorry but I don't have the energy to celebrate with you at this moment. I can't switch my emotions that quickly." I thought to myself, *how inconsiderate to dismiss my sorrow and choose to brag at such a moment about how great your life is.* No sympathy or empathy whatsoever. One can mistake her actions as kicking you while you're on the floor, half-dead. I will conclude she doesn't know better, for argument's sake.

After I was released from the mental health facility, Virginia bragged that she was such a great friend, because she does so much for me. *She sure knows how to toot her own horn as well as others.* Proverbs 27:2 says, "Let another praise you, and not your own mouth." This keeps us humble. I stopped her mid-conversation and told her, "I'm sorry, but whatever you do for me is because you want to. Not because I asked you to." I don't ever remind people what I have done for them because I don't seek recognition. It makes me feel good to help others. I told her, "That is exactly why I prefer people not helping me. I don't need it to be thrown back in my face. I'd rather do for others than to receive anything in return." I didn't even bother to remind her we took an eight-year break from one another because of her selfishness. She was a taker and I was a giver and she burnt me out.

Her words of flattery held our friendship together. My self-esteem was so low, I needed words of praise. In Proverbs 29:5 "Whoever flatters his neighbor is spreading a net for his feet." I totally fell into the trap of feeding my insecurity. Once I felt the imbalance of the relationship after having a one-year-old who also required 100% of me, I dropped our relationship. I let her know she took advantage of my kindness by citing several examples of her actions. Surprisingly, Virginia admitted she was guilty of each of those actions. I was shocked she is so self-aware.

She then recalled an incident where one of her students asked, "Do you want anything for lunch from McDonalds?" Her response was, "Sure, can you get me a taco from Taco Bell?" Therefore, I wasn't her only victim. She was constantly pushing people's boundaries and knew the person was willing to go out of their way. I was dumbfounded by her acknowledgement that she is fully aware of her actions. I take full responsibility for allowing such behavior in my life. That is when I parted ways from her. As much as I knew it wasn't healthy to continue the friendship, I missed her. When she came back into my life eight years later, she tried to manipulate me again but she couldn't because I had just read the book *Boundaries*. Virginia shared her gratitude with me that I left our relationship because she has learned to be a giver and she would like to give back to me. *Wow, she wanted to reciprocate.* I wasn't used to reciprocal friendships in my life. At first, she tried to ask for unreasonable favors and I was able to practice my "No" or redirect her to another solution. I didn't want to become her babysitter or her uber driver in the middle of the night. I let her know to use the daycare after school and download the uber app. She respected my responses.

Now was the perfect time to tell her, "I'm sorry you may think you're a good friend to me, nor did I ever want to tell you this; when I needed you most, you were not there for me. You didn't open your doors when I didn't have a place to live." She didn't even know how to respond. She quickly learned not to throw in my face anything she does for me. We should only be doing for people unto God. Our recognition should come from God and God alone. Matthew 6:4 tells us, "so that your giving may be in secret. Then your Father, who sees what is done in secret, will reward you." Never brag about what you do for people because then you cheat yourself from God's gift.

It is easy to have friends in the good times, but are they there for you when you need them the most? No one can manipulate God. We should respect ourselves the same way. Many who have heard of Jesus may say, "Lord, Lord!" Don't be surprised if God responds, "I never knew you; depart from me, you who practice lawlessness!" On judgment day, many will look for God, and say we prophesied in your name and cast out demons in your name, and done many wonders in your name. Another great example of how good deeds do not bring eternal life. They will not be recognized for their evil ways as told in Matthew 7:22-23. It clearly states in Luke 6:46, "Why do you call me, 'Lord, Lord,' and do not do what I say?" God wants to be heard, respected and loved just like we all do. It's that simple to have an amazing relationship with him. The same is true for giving. It's easy to be generous when you have plenty, but how about when you have limited funds?

Giving when you don't have is more meaningful. In John 12, Mary poured a pint of expensive perfume on Jesus' feet and brushed the fragrance with her hair. But Judas, one of Jesus' disciples, didn't like what Mary did. Judas felt the perfume was wasted because it could have been sold or given to the poor. The perfume was worth a year's pay. Judas didn't care about the poor because he was a thief. Jesus replied, "leave her alone the perfume was meant for the day I will be buried." Mary had a giving heart. I may not have much, but I want to be just as generous.

Two days later, I received a call from a blocked number on my phone. I pick it up and it was Virginia ready to attack me,

"What was that email you sent me all about?" I was thinking, *Wow, she is going to attempt this route with me?* I calmly asked, "Which part didn't you understand?" She couldn't answer that question. She proceeded to attack me because she was caught off guard. She rudely tells me, "Why couldn't you call me to talk about it?" I asked, "What difference does it make? Now you want to deflect and make this about how I'm supposed to express myself. Because of this exact scenario, I didn't contact you by phone because you're quick to attack." I asked her, "What do you think you are going to accomplish by talking to me in that tone of voice you're using and the attitude you're giving me right now?" I knew she couldn't answer that either. I said, "I'm sorry but I'm hanging up." Wow, I've come a long way. This was a conversation I avoided for a long time and I'm proud that I finally realized this relationship adds no value to my life. She offered me an abundance of flattering words that I no longer needed from her. I can now tell myself my own truths of affirmation. I felt a sense of freedom.

By the end of the night, I received an email from Virginia. It seemed as though someone helped her write the email. It read, *Ava, I am saddened by what is transpiring between us. I have reread your email and am truly sorry that you feel that way. My intentions were not to hurt you. Take as long as you need to. Always keeping you in my thoughts and prayers. Be well.* My response to her was, *Much better, Virginia. Sounds sincere. I don't want to feel attacked, because the only person who should be angry is me and I'm sincerely not. I overlook many things but God revealed to me Proverbs 27:5-6, "An open rebuke is better than hidden love." Also Proverbs 28:23 says, In the end, people appreciate honest criticism far more than flattery. I accept your apology but will still like to have my space. I'm sure by the New Year, I will be in a better place. I'm just taking a sabbatical from everyone from New York until then. Thank you. I need all the prayers I can get.* I know we are all a work in progress but space is where we grow.

Embrace the Judas in your life. Don't try to avoid them or repel them. There is always a silver lining in our circumstances. Matthew 5:43-44 says, "You have heard that it was said, 'love your neighbor and hate your enemy.' But I tell you: Love your enemies and pray for those who persecute you." You are building character with confidence to know who you truly are in Christ, seeking no one's approval but God alone.

CHAPTER SEVENTEEN

HOW CAN I FIND FORGIVENESS EVEN WHEN IT'S NOT MY FAULT?

I emailed Robert to see if he would allow the boys to visit me in Florida for Christmas. I figured Robert and his sister could visit their mother who lives in Florida as well. We don't know how much more time Robert's mom has here on earth, as tomorrow is never promised to us. I wouldn't have been surprised if Robert didn't know where she lived either. He had never visited her before. He responded saying, "You tried to take everything from me!" That was the lie he was telling himself. Seems like he just wanted to stay angry. His actions forced me to leave the marriage. He was the one who got the order of protection against me when I eloped the hospital. He also changed the door locks to our home so I couldn't return. I suppose he forgot he didn't own anything when I first met him. He had no car and bad credit. His name on my credit cards improved his score as I responsibly made my own payments. I never rendered the credit cards to him.

Now I'm dealing with a self-entitled person. It amazes me, how you think you know someone to discover they're not who they pretended to be. I never knew I was *Sleeping with the Enemy*. That was a great movie. He forgot I tried to offer him $45k because that was all I had saved in the past two years, living at my parents' house. I told him, I would rather give him the money than the attorneys whose charged $500 per hour. He turned my offer down. He may have thought he was on Shark Tank TV series with entrepreneurs who present their breakthrough business concepts. His eyes were bigger because he wanted it all: money, house and kids. This man doesn't even realize he took everything from me. Robert left me homeless and took away my children. Now I have to speak irrationally to get relational.

I have forgiven Robert, but this time I decided to try something different. I decided to ask Robert to forgive me because my intentions were never to hurt him. I know asking him to forgive me sounds insane but I was not dealing with a sane person. Don't get mad, readers, like most of my acquaintances did when I told them this. I had to explain, this doesn't mean I wanted to reconcile with him. This doesn't mean I want a friendship. This only means I want to be respected with proper boundaries in place because of the children. I'm desperate to see my boys, and this tactic is something I hadn't tried. I just want peace with their dad. Different actions usually bring different results. He never replied. I think he didn't know how to respond. At least I didn't get his insane emails with no logic. I've tried asking for friendship for the sake of the children. I have asked him to join us if he felt more comfortable extending the time I have with my children. He was also welcome to include his girlfriend on the visit. I just needed him to loosen his guarded walls of anger because I love my children. I don't want to wait till my children are 18 years old when they can make their own decisions.

It's okay if most people don't agree with me apologizing. I just know I only need God to agree with me. I didn't deserve to be forgiven when God forgave me. In Matthew 18:21-22, "Peter came to Jesus and asked, "Lord, how many times shall I forgive my brother when he sins against me? Up to seven times?" Jesus answered, "I tell you, not seven times, but seventy-seven times?" Just set proper boundaries. For those of you who think I was the victim, I wasn't because no one can take my peace from me. I always remember my Bible verse Luke 23:34, "Forgive them

> WHO CAN YOU FORGIVE TODAY? OR DO YOU STRUGGLE TO FORGIVEN YOURSELF. ASK GOD TO HELP YOU TO FORGIVE IF YOUR NOT SURE HOW.

for they do not know." Robert is the victim because he is holding onto anger. I'm just thankful for my trials and tribulations, because without the storms I can't grow my character to be more like Jesus.

I will hold tight onto God's promise in Joel 2:25, "I will repay you for the years the locusts have eaten, the cankerworm, and the caterpillar, and the Palmer worm, my great army which I sent among you." I know my blessings are around the corner. I trust the Lord will reunite me again with my children one day in such a lavish way. My sweet Jesus wants to give me an abundant life of joy, love, and peace.

I told Louis, I was praying he would be able to visit me in Florida for Christmas. Louis shared with me that their Aunt Julie is trying to get her ill mother Lola to travel to New York for Christmas instead. Therefore, Louis didn't think they would come to Florida for the holiday. In my heart, I know their dad didn't deny me either. Julie is relentless with her tactics to keep me from seeing my children. For a split minute my heart wanted to burst out of my chest. Then I rationalized with God again and said,

"That's okay, God. Your plans are greater," and I reflected on Proverbs 16:9, "The heart of man plans his way, but the Lord establishes his steps." Julie is relentless in making sure I don't see my children. I'm completely removed from her life and don't see the motive behind her actions. I removed the bitterness from my heart immediately and said to myself, *she can plan whatever she wants.* I know my God has the last say. So, Lord, "I am looking forward to Christmas with my children whatever you think is forthcoming." I'm so impressed how quickly I can pacify my mind because of the Holy Spirit within me. Needless to say, I didn't see my boys for Christmas. I still give thanks because I know the enemy cannot trip me thoughts towards anger.

Now I attract healthy friendships, adding value to my life without an agenda and with a sincere heart. Proverbs 27:17, "As iron sharpens iron, so one person sharpens another." I thank God for my new attraction. I didn't realize how many more people were struggling with similar situations from my past circumstance. When I shifted my thinking, I said to myself, *I don't need people to like me, people don't have to believe me and I don't have to be self-reliant. God is going to fight my battles as promised in Deuteronomy 3:22.* The raider of controlling friendships no longer pursues me. It was such a pleasure to build new friendships where both are conscious not to intentionally take advantage of each other. You are more respected when you're honest with yourself and

WHAT BRANCHES NEED TO BE PRUNED WITHIN YOURSELF?

others. My storm is my happiness to liberation. This was all part of God's pruning.

The storms in our lives help us to grow. We need to be watered and fertilized by the storm to stand tall. Are you growing? What lessons have you learned in the ever-changing weathers of life?

I'm thankful Robert subconsciously taught me to set proper boundaries by forcing me to leave the marriage. I probably wouldn't have the courage to do it on my own. I remember telling him in court, "Why are you so angry? I did you a favor, you weren't in love with me." He couldn't answer. I have asked Robert if we could maintain a respectful cordial relationship for the sake of the children. He ignored my request. I've pleaded with him to take supervision off. He ignored my request. I will do whatever it takes to maintain peace between us so I can see my children. I did love Robert. I have no regrets. He is the father of my children and I only wish Robert to be happier with his new life.

Who said bipolar is incurable? I've found so many articles online that state there is no cure for bipolar disorder. Yes, through behavioral therapy and the right combination of mood stabilizers, the illness can be controlled. I am not against medication. For me, extensive therapy to get to the root of the triggers in my life was my cure. I don't allow feelings to dictate my emotions any longer. Self-awareness, proper sleep, eating healthy, journaling, prayers, exercising and not bottling up my trauma were my healing ingredients; not medication. The nights I can't sleep, I ask God, "What should we discuss? I'm sorry if I left you out of my day! Let's talk. You have my full attention." I take my concerns to him as my mighty counselor and healer.

Most importantly replacing lies with God's truth is so liberating. I remind myself, "I was created in his image," Genesis 1:26, "For we are God's masterpiece," Ephesians 2:10. Thank you Lord for healing my bipolar disorder.

I would love to hear your thoughts about this book and what lessons in my story you can apply to your life? We welcome your reviews online. Your honest feedback matters to us.

Subscribe to www.wigboutique.com or www.denisetorres.org to stay connected for future book releases.

Made in the USA
Monee, IL
12 September 2022

039f04f5-4111-464f-bff5-46b1e14a7c18R04